Fortnite Cookbook

Unofficial

Contents

Desserts

Beverages

Starters

Cheesy Rainbow Bagels

Get ready for an explosion of colors and flavors! Inspired by the vibrant and dynamic world of Fortnite, these Cheesy Rainbow Bagels are a feast for the eyes and the taste buds. With their bright and eye-catching colors, each bite brings you a delightful burst of cheesy goodness. Perfect for breakfast or as a fun snack.

Ingredients:

For the Bagels:

- 4 cups (480 g) bread flour, plus extra for kneading
- 2 teaspoons (10 g) salt
- 2 teaspoons (10 g) instant yeast
- 1 1/2 cups (360 ml) warm water
- 2 tablespoons (30 g) granulated sugar
- Food coloring (red, orange, yellow, green, blue, purple)

For the Water Bath:

- 8 cups (1.9 liters) water
- 2 tablespoons (30 g) granulated sugar
- 1 tablespoon (15 g) baking soda

For Serving:

- 8 ounces (225 g) cream cheese
- Food coloring (optional, to match bagels)

Instructions:

-In a large bowl, combine the bread flour, salt, and instant yeast.

-Add the warm water and mix until a dough forms.

-Knead the dough on a floured surface for about 10 minutes

-Divide the dough into 6 equal parts and place each portion

-Add a few drops of food coloring to each bowl, one color per bowl.

-Knead each portion until the color is evenly distributed, adding more food coloring as needed to achieve vibrant colors.

-Roll each colored dough portion into a long rope, about 12 inches (30 cm) long.

-Lay the ropes side by side and gently press them together.

-Twist the combined ropes together and then roll them into a single, longer rope.

-Divide the twisted rope into 8 equal pieces and shape each piece into a bagel by connecting the ends together.

-Place the shaped bagels on a baking sheet lined with parchment paper.

-Cover them with a damp towel and let them rise for about 20 minutes.

-In a large pot, bring 8 cups of water to a boil.

-Add the granulated sugar and baking soda, and reduce to a simmer.

-Carefully drop 2-3 bagels at a time into the simmering water.

-Boil each bagel for 1 minute on each side, then remove them with a slotted spoon and place them back on the parchment-lined baking sheet.

Bake the bagels in the preheated oven 425°F (220°C) for 20-25 minutes.

-Spread the cream cheese on each bagel and enjoy!

Dusty Depot Dip

This warm, cheesy dip is packed with vegetables and rich flavors, making it the perfect party appetizer or game-time snack. Featuring a creamy blend of artichokes, spinach, and a mix of cheeses, each bite is a delicious reminder of the iconic in-game location. Serve it hot with tortilla chips, crackers, or sliced baguette for a winning combination that will leave everyone asking for more. Dive into this epic dip and bring the taste of Dusty Depot to your table!

Ingredients:

For the Dip:

- 2 tablespoons (30 ml) olive oil
- 1 small onion, finely chopped
- 3 cloves garlic, minced
- 1 can (14 ounces / 400 g) artichoke hearts, drained and chopped
- 1 package (10 ounces / 280 g) frozen chopped spinach, thawed and drained
- 8 ounces (225 g) cream cheese, softened
- 1/2 cup (120 ml) sour cream
- 1/4 cup (60 ml) mayonnaise
- 1 cup (100 g) grated Parmesan cheese
- 1 cup (100 g) shredded mozzarella cheese
- 1 teaspoon (5 g) red pepper flakes (optional for extra heat)
- Salt and pepper to taste

For Serving:

- Tortilla chips
- Crackers

Instructions:

1.Prepare the Vegetables:

-In a large skillet, heat the olive oil over medium heat.

-Add the finely chopped onion and sauté until translucent, about 5 minutes.

-Add the minced garlic and cook for an additional minute until fragrant.

2.Combine the Artichoke and Spinach:

-Stir in the chopped artichoke hearts and the drained, thawed spinach.

-Cook for another 2-3 minutes, mixing well to combine and heat

3.Prepare the Creamy Base:

-Reduce the heat to low and add the softened cream cheese to the skillet.

-Stir until the cream cheese is melted and well incorporated with the vegetables.

-Add the sour cream and mayonnaise, mixing until smooth.

4.Add the Cheeses:

-Stir in the grated Parmesan cheese and half of the shredded mozzarella cheese.

-Add the red pepper flakes if using, and season with salt and pepper to taste.

5.Transfer to Baking Dish:

-Preheat your oven to 375°F (190°C).

-Transfer the mixture to a baking dish and spread it out evenly.

-Sprinkle the remaining shredded mozzarella cheese on top.

Bake in the preheated oven for 20-25 minutes

7.Serve.

Mango Moshpit Salsa

Add a burst of tropical flavor to your table with Mango Moshpit Salsa. This refreshing salsa combines sweet, juicy mangoes with the crisp crunch of red bell pepper and the zesty kick of jalapeño, all brought together with fresh lime juice and cilantro. Perfect as a dip for tortilla chips or a topping for grilled meats and fish, this salsa will bring a lively moshpit of flavors to any gathering.

Ingredients:

- 2 ripe mangoes, peeled, pitted, and diced
- 1 red bell pepper, diced
- 1/2 red onion, finely chopped
- 1 jalapeño, seeded and finely chopped
- 1/4 cup (60 ml) fresh cilantro, chopped
- 1/4 cup (60 ml) fresh lime juice (about 2 limes)
- 1 tablespoon (15 ml) olive oil
- Salt and pepper to taste

Instructions:

1.Prepare the Ingredients:

-Peel, pit, and dice the mangoes. Place them in a large mixing bowl.

-Dice the red bell pepper and finely chop the red onion. Add them to the bowl with the mangoes.

-Finely chop the jalapeño, removing the seeds for less heat. Add it to the bowl.

-Chop the fresh cilantro and add it to the bowl.

2.Mix the Salsa:

-Pour the fresh lime juice and olive oil over the mango mixture.

-Gently toss all the ingredients together until well combined.

3.Season and Serve:

-Season with salt and pepper to taste.

-Serve immediately or refrigerate for an hour to allow the flavors to meld.

Paradise Palms Pita

Transport yourself to the sun-soaked sands of Paradise Palms with this Mediterranean Chicken Pita. Juicy, marinated chicken infused with aromatic spices is perfectly complemented by creamy hummus, fresh veggies, and tangy feta cheese. Topped with a refreshing homemade tzatziki sauce, this dish is perfect for a quick lunch or a lively dinner gathering. Enjoy a taste of the Mediterranean that will keep you coming back for more.

Ingredients:

- 1 pound (450 g) boneless, skinless chicken breasts or thighs
- 1/4 cup (60 ml) olive oil
- Juice of 1 lemon
- 3 cloves garlic, minced
- 1 teaspoon (5 g) dried oregano
- 1 teaspoon (5 g) ground cumin
- 1 teaspoon (5 g) smoked paprika
- 1/2 teaspoon (2.5 g) salt
- 1/2 teaspoon (2.5 g) black pepper
- 4 whole wheat or white pita bread
- 1 cup (240 ml) hummus
- 1 cup (150 g) cherry tomatoes, halved
- 1 cucumber, diced
- 1/4 cup (40 g) red onion, thinly sliced
- 1/2 cup (75 g) crumbled feta cheese
- 1/4 cup (60 ml) pitted Kalamata olives,
- Fresh parsley or mint leaves
- 1 cup (240 ml) Greek yogurt
- 1/2 cucumber
- 1 tablespoon (15 ml) lemon juice
- 1 tablespoon (15 ml) olive oil
- 2 cloves garlic, minced
- 1 tablespoon (15 g) fresh dill, chopped

Instructions:

1.Marinate the Chicken:

-In a bowl, combine olive oil, lemon juice, minced garlic, dried oregano, ground cumin, smoked paprika, salt, and black pepper.

-Add the chicken breasts or thighs to the marinade, ensuring they are well coated. Cover and refrigerate for at least 30 minutes, or up to 4 hours for best results.

2.Cook the Chicken:

-Preheat your grill or a skillet over medium-high heat.

-Grill or cook the marinated chicken for 5-7 minutes on each side, or until the internal temperature reaches 165°F (74°C) and the chicken is cooked through.

-Remove from heat and let it rest for a few minutes before slicing into thin strips.

3.Prepare the Tzatziki Sauce:

-In a bowl, combine Greek yogurt, grated cucumber, lemon juice, olive oil, minced garlic, and chopped fresh dill. Mix well.

-Season with salt and pepper to taste. Refrigerate until ready to use.

4.Assemble the Pitas:

-Warm the pita bread in a dry skillet or microwave to make them pliable.

-Spread a generous amount of hummus inside each pita pocket.

-Add the sliced chicken, cherry tomatoes, diced cucumber, thinly sliced red onion, crumbled feta cheese, and sliced Kalamata olives.

5.Add the Tzatziki Sauce.

6.Garnish and Serve.

Retail Row Ramen

Step into the bustling marketplace of Retail Row with this flavorful ramen. It features tender, caramelized pork marinated in a blend of soy sauce, mirin, and spices, then roasted to perfection. Paired with a rich and savory broth, this ramen is elevated with fresh vegetables, soft-boiled eggs, and classic toppings like nori strips and sesame seeds.

Ingredients:

•1 pound (450 g) pork shoulder or belly
•2 tablespoons (30 ml) soy sauce
•2 tablespoons (30 ml) mirin
•2 tablespoons (30 g) brown sugar
•2 cloves garlic, minced
•1 teaspoon (5 g) grated ginger
•1 tablespoon (15 ml) sesame oil
•1 tablespoon (15 ml) sriracha
•4 cups (1 liter) chicken or pork broth
•2 tablespoons (30 ml) soy sauce
•2 tablespoons (30 ml) miso paste
•1 tablespoon (15 ml) fish sauce
•1 tablespoon (15 ml) rice vinegar
•1 tablespoon (15 ml) sesame oil
•1 teaspoon (5 g) grated ginger
•4 servings of ramen noodles
•4 soft-boiled eggs, halved
•1 cup (150 g) baby spinach
•1 cup (150 g) bean sprouts
•1/2 cup (75 g) corn kernels
•2 green onions, thinly sliced
•1 sheet nori (seaweed), cut into strips
•1 tablespoon (15 g) sesame seeds

Instructions:

1.Prepare the Pork:

-In a bowl, combine soy sauce, mirin, brown sugar, minced garlic, grated ginger, sesame oil, and sriracha (or chili garlic sauce).

-Place the pork shoulder or pork belly in a resealable bag or a shallow dish and pour the marinade over the pork. Marinate for at least 30 minutes, or preferably overnight in the refrigerator.

2.Cook the Pork:

-Preheat your oven to 350°F (175°C).

-Place the marinated pork on a baking sheet lined with foil or parchment paper.

-Roast the pork for 1.5 to 2 hours, or until it is tender and caramelized. Baste the pork occasionally with the marinade during cooking.

-Let the pork rest for a few minutes, then slice it thinly.

3.Prepare the Broth:

-In a large pot, combine the chicken or pork broth, water, soy sauce, miso paste, fish sauce, rice vinegar, sesame oil, grated ginger, minced garlic, and dried shiitake mushrooms (if using).

-Bring the broth to a boil, then reduce the heat and let it simmer for 15-20 minutes to allow the flavors to meld together.

-Remove the dried shiitake mushrooms before serving.

4.Cook the Ramen Noodles:

-Cook the ramen noodles according to the package instructions. Drain and set aside.

5.Assemble the Ramen Bowls and serve.

Sniper's Snack Fries

These crispy, golden fries are seasoned to perfection with a blend of garlic, paprika, and thyme, then baked until irresistibly crunchy. As you patiently wait for your target, indulge in this savory treat topped with Parmesan cheese, fresh herbs, and a drizzle of truffle oil for a gourmet touch. Perfect for gaming nights or as a delicious side, these fries will keep your energy and focus sharp for any battle.

Ingredients:

For the Fries:

- 4 large russet potatoes
- 2-3 tablespoons (30-45 ml) vegetable oil
- 1 teaspoon (5 g) salt
- 1/2 teaspoon (2.5 g) black pepper
- 1 teaspoon (5 g) garlic powder
- 1 teaspoon (5 g) paprika
- 1/2 teaspoon (2.5 g) dried thyme

For the Toppings:

- 1/2 cup (60 g) grated Parmesan cheese
- 2 tablespoons (30 ml) fresh parsley, chopped
- 1 tablespoon (15 ml) fresh rosemary, chopped
- Truffle oil (optional)
- Aioli or garlic mayo (optional for dipping)
- Ketchup (optional for dipping)

Instructions:

1.Prepare the Potatoes:

-Preheat your oven to 425°F (220°C).

-Wash and peel the potatoes. Cut them into thin, uniform sticks (about 1/4 inch thick).

-Soak the potato sticks in a bowl of cold water for at least 30 minutes to remove excess starch. Drain and pat them dry with a clean kitchen towel or paper towels.

2.Season the Fries:

-In a large bowl, toss the dried potato sticks with vegetable oil, ensuring they are evenly coated.

-Sprinkle the salt, black pepper, garlic powder, paprika, and dried thyme over the potatoes. Toss again to evenly distribute the seasoning.

3.Bake the Fries:

-Arrange the seasoned potato sticks in a single layer on a baking sheet lined with parchment paper. Do not overcrowd the pan; use two baking sheets if necessary.

-Bake in the preheated oven for 25-30 minutes, flipping the fries halfway through, until they are golden brown and crispy.

4.Add the Gourmet Touch:

-While the fries are still hot, sprinkle the grated Parmesan cheese, chopped fresh parsley, and chopped fresh rosemary over them.

-Drizzle with truffle oil if using, for an extra gourmet touch.

5.Serve.

Stealthy Stronghold Garlic Bread

Perfect for snacking while strategizing or lying in wait, this garlic bread is a savory delight that's both crunchy and soft. Infused with rich garlic butter and topped with a blend of herbs and Parmesan cheese, each bite is a burst of flavor. Whether you're hiding out or charging into action, this garlic bread will give you the boost you need to conquer any challenge.

6-8 servings
Difficulty:
Easy

Ingredients:

•1 loaf of French bread or Italian bread
•1/2 cup (115 g) unsalted butter, softened
•4 cloves garlic, minced
•1/4 cup (25 g) grated Parmesan cheese
•2 tablespoons (30 ml) fresh parsley, chopped
•1 teaspoon (5 g) salt
•1/2 teaspoon (2.5 g) black pepper
•Optional: 1/2 teaspoon (2.5 g) dried oregano or dried basil
•Optional: shredded mozzarella cheese for topping

Instructions:

1.Preheat the Oven:
-Preheat your oven to 375°F (190°C).
2.Prepare the Bread:
-Slice the loaf of bread in half lengthwise. Place the halves on a baking sheet, cut side up.
3.Make the Garlic Butter:
oIn a medium bowl, combine the softened butter, minced garlic, grated Parmesan cheese, chopped parsley, salt, and black pepper. If using, add the dried oregano or dried basil. Mix until well combined.
4.Spread the Garlic Butter:
-Evenly spread the garlic butter mixture over the cut sides of the bread halves.
5.Optional Cheese Topping:
oIf desired, sprinkle shredded mozzarella cheese evenly over the garlic butter.
6.Bake the Garlic Bread:
-Place the baking sheet in the preheated oven and bake for 10-15 minutes, or until the bread is golden and crispy, and the cheese (if using) is melted and bubbly.
7.Serve:
-Remove the garlic bread from the oven and let it cool for a few minutes.
-Slice the bread into pieces and serve warm.

Storm Circle Rings

Get ready to brave the storm with these crispy, golden Storm Circle Onion Rings, inspired by Fortnite's ever-shrinking battlefield. Perfect for snacking while navigating the chaos, these onion rings are coated in a seasoned batter and fried to crunchy perfection. Each ring offers a satisfying crunch followed by a burst of savory onion flavor.

Ingredients:

- 2 large onions, sliced into 1/4-inch (0.6 cm) rings
- 2 cups (240 g) all-purpose flour, divided
- 1 teaspoon (5 g) baking powder
- 1 teaspoon (5 g) salt
- 1/2 teaspoon (2.5 g) paprika
- 1/2 teaspoon (2.5 g) black pepper
- 1 cup (240 ml) buttermilk
- 1 cup (240 ml) cold water
- Vegetable oil for frying

Instructions:

1.Prepare the Onion Rings:

-Separate the sliced onions into individual rings and set aside.

2.Prepare the Batter:

-In a large bowl, whisk together 1 1/2 cups (180 g) of the flour, baking powder, salt, paprika, and black pepper.

-Add the buttermilk and cold water to the flour mixture, whisking until smooth.

3.Prepare the Dry Dredge:

-Place the remaining 1/2 cup (60 g) of flour in a shallow dish.

4.Heat the Oil:

-In a deep frying pan or pot, heat vegetable oil to 350°F (175°C). The oil should be about 2 inches (5 cm) deep.

5.Dredge and Batter the Onion Rings:

-Working in batches, dredge the onion rings in the dry flour, shaking off any excess.

-Dip the floured onion rings into the batter, allowing any excess to drip off.

6.Fry the Onion Rings:

-Carefully place the battered onion rings into the hot oil. Fry for about 2-3 minutes per side, or until golden brown and crispy.

-Use a slotted spoon to remove the onion rings from the oil and drain on paper towels.

7.Serve.

Storm's Eye Soup

Prepare to weather any storm with Storm's Eye Soup, a hearty and nourishing dish inspired by Fortnite's intense final circles. This robust soup is packed with nutrient-rich vegetables, lentils, and a medley of spices, creating a comforting blend that's perfect for keeping your focus and energy high. With the addition of fresh greens and a bright splash of lemon juice, each bowl delivers a well-rounded flavor profile that will keep you ready for action. Garnish with fresh parsley and enjoy this storm-proof meal, perfect for any culinary battleground.

Ingredients:

•2 tablespoons (30 ml) olive oil

•1 large onion, diced

•2 cloves garlic, minced

•3 carrots, diced

•3 celery stalks, diced

•1 large potato, diced

•1 cup (200 g) dried green or brown lentils, rinsed

•1 can (14.5 ounces / 400 g) diced tomatoes

•6 cups (1.5 liters) vegetable broth

•1 teaspoon (5 g) ground cumin

•1 teaspoon (5 g) ground coriander

•1/2 teaspoon (2.5 g) smoked paprika

•1/2 teaspoon (2.5 g) turmeric

•Salt and pepper to taste

•1 bay leaf

•2 cups (60 g) chopped kale or spinach

•Juice of 1 lemon

•Fresh parsley for garnish

Instructions:

1.Prepare the Vegetables:

-Dice the onion, carrots, celery, and potato. Mince the garlic.

2.Sauté the Aromatics:

-In a large pot, heat the olive oil over medium heat.

-Add the diced onion and sauté until it becomes translucent, about 5 minutes.

-Add the minced garlic and cook for another minute until fragrant.

3.Add the Vegetables:

-Add the diced carrots, celery, and potato to the pot. Cook for about 5-7 minutes, stirring occasionally, until the vegetables begin to soften.

4.Add the Lentils and Spices:

-Stir in the rinsed lentils, ground cumin, ground coriander, smoked paprika, turmeric, salt, and pepper. Mix well to coat the vegetables and lentils with the spices.

5.Add the Tomatoes and Broth:

-Pour in the can of diced tomatoes and the vegetable broth.

-Add the bay leaf and bring the soup to a boil.

6.Simmer the Soup:

-Reduce the heat to low, cover the pot, and let the soup simmer for about 30-35 minutes, or until the lentils and vegetables are tender.

7.Add the Greens:

-Stir in the chopped kale or spinach and cook for an additional 5 minutes until the greens are wilted and tender.

8.Finish with Lemon.

Team Zesty Lemon Rice

Join forces with flavor with Team Zesty Lemon Rice, a dish that brings a bright and tangy twist to your mealtime, inspired by the camaraderie and spirit of Fortnite's team play. This vibrant rice dish combines fluffy basmati rice with the zest and juice of fresh lemons, complemented by aromatic herbs and spices. Perfect as a side dish or a light main, this recipe is sure to elevate any meal with its refreshing and zesty profile.

Ingredients:

•1 cup (200 g) basmati rice
•2 cups (480 ml) water
•1/4 cup (60 ml) fresh lemon juice
•Zest of 1 lemon
•2 tablespoons (30 ml) vegetable oil
•1/2 teaspoon (2.5 g) mustard seeds
•1/2 teaspoon (2.5 g) cumin seeds
•1/4 teaspoon (1.25 g) turmeric powder
•1/4 teaspoon (1.25 g) asafoetida (hing) (optional)
•2 tablespoons (30 g) roasted peanuts or cashews
•2 green chilies, slit lengthwise
•1 sprig curry leaves (optional)
•Salt to taste
•Fresh cilantro, chopped (for garnish)

Instructions:

1.Cook the Rice:

-Rinse the basmati rice under cold water until the water runs clear.

-In a medium saucepan, bring 2 cups of water to a boil.

-Add the rinsed rice and a pinch of salt, then reduce the heat to low, cover, and simmer for about 15 minutes, or until the rice is cooked and the water is absorbed.

-Remove from heat and let the rice sit, covered, for 5 minutes. Fluff with a fork and set aside to cool.

2.Prepare the Seasoning:

-In a large pan or wok, heat the vegetable oil over medium heat.

-Add the mustard seeds and cumin seeds. Let them sizzle and pop for a few seconds.

-Add the turmeric powder and asafoetida (if using). Stir briefly.

-Add the roasted peanuts or cashews, slit green chilies, and curry leaves (if using). Sauté for 2-3 minutes until the peanuts or cashews are lightly browned and the curry leaves are crisp.

3.Combine the Rice and Seasoning:

-Add the cooked rice to the pan and gently mix to combine with the seasoning.

-Pour the fresh lemon juice over the rice and add the lemon zest. Mix well to ensure the rice is evenly coated with the lemon juice.

-Season with salt to taste.

4.Serve:

-Garnish the lemon rice with chopped fresh cilantro.

Vibe Gazpacho

Cool down and stay refreshed with Vibe Gazpacho, inspired by the chill and relaxed atmosphere of Fortnite's most laid-back locales. This vibrant, cold soup is bursting with the fresh flavors of ripe tomatoes, crisp cucumbers, bell peppers, and garlic, blended to perfection and chilled for ultimate refreshment. Ideal for hot days and intense gaming sessions, this gazpacho is not only easy to prepare but also a nutritious way to stay hydrated and energized. Serve it chilled and let the vibes carry you to victory.

Ingredients:

- 6 large ripe tomatoes, cored and chopped
- 1 large cucumber, peeled, seeded, and chopped
- 1 red bell pepper, chopped
- 1 green bell pepper, chopped
- 1 small red onion, chopped
- 3 cloves garlic, minced
- 2 cups (480 ml) tomato juice
- 1/4 cup (60 ml) extra-virgin olive oil
- 3 tablespoons (45 ml) red wine vinegar
- 1 tablespoon (15 ml) lemon juice
- 1 teaspoon (5 g) salt
- 1/2 teaspoon (2.5 g) black pepper
- 1/2 teaspoon (2.5 g) smoked paprika (optional)
- 1/4 teaspoon (1.25 g) cayenne pepper (optional)
- Fresh basil or parsley, chopped (for garnish)

Instructions:

1.Prepare the Vegetables:

-In a large bowl, combine the chopped tomatoes, cucumber, red bell pepper, green bell pepper, red onion, and minced garlic.

2.Blend the Gazpacho:

-In batches, transfer the vegetable mixture to a blender or food processor and blend until smooth. You can blend it to your desired consistency, either completely smooth or slightly chunky.

3.Combine and Season:

-Pour the blended mixture back into the large bowl. Add the tomato juice, extra-virgin olive oil, red wine vinegar, lemon juice, salt, black pepper, smoked paprika (if using), and cayenne pepper (if using). Stir well to combine.

4.Chill the Gazpacho:

-Cover the bowl and refrigerate the gazpacho for at least 2 hours, or until well chilled. The flavors will meld and develop as it chills.

5.Serve:

-Stir the gazpacho before serving. Taste and adjust the seasoning if necessary.

-Ladle the chilled gazpacho into bowls or glasses.

-Garnish with chopped fresh basil or parsley.

Main dishes

LIS

Battle Bus Burrito

Packed with seasoned beef, beans, fresh vegetables, and melty cheese, this burrito is a powerhouse of flavors and textures. Whether you're gearing up for a big game or need a satisfying meal on the go, this burrito has got you covered. Easy to make and even easier to enjoy, it's the perfect fuel for any battle.

Ingredients:

•2 tablespoons (30 ml) olive oil

•1 pound (450 g) boneless, skinless chicken breasts

•1 large onion, diced

•2 cloves garlic, minced

•1 bell pepper, diced

•1 teaspoon (5 g) ground cumin

•1 teaspoon (5 g) chili powder

•1/2 teaspoon (2.5 g) smoked paprika

•1/2 teaspoon (2.5 g) black pepper

•1 can (15 ounces / 425 g) black beans, drained and rinsed

•1 cup (240 ml) corn kernels (fresh, frozen, or canned)

•1 cup (240 ml) salsa

•1/4 cup (60 ml) chopped fresh cilantro

•Juice of 1 lime

•8 large flour tortillas

•1 1/2 cups (180 g) shredded cheddar or Monterey Jack cheese

•1 cup (240 ml) cooked rice (optional)

•1 cup (240 ml) shredded lettuce

•1/2 cup (120 ml) sour cream

•1/2 cup (120 ml) guacamole

Instructions:

1.Prepare the Burrito Filling:

-In a large skillet, heat the olive oil over medium-high heat.

-Add the diced chicken and cook until browned and cooked through, about 5-7 minutes. Remove the chicken from the skillet and set aside.

-In the same skillet, add the diced onion and bell pepper. Sauté for 4-5 minutes until softened.

-Add the minced garlic, ground cumin, chili powder, smoked paprika, salt, and black pepper. Cook for an additional 1-2 minutes until fragrant.

-Stir in the black beans, corn kernels, and salsa. Cook for another 3-4 minutes until heated through.

-Return the cooked chicken to the skillet and mix well to combine.

-Stir in the chopped cilantro and lime juice. Remove from heat.

2.Assemble the Burritos:

-Warm the flour tortillas in a dry skillet or microwave to make them pliable.

-Lay out each tortilla on a flat surface. In the center of each tortilla, add a portion of the chicken and black bean filling.

-Sprinkle with shredded cheese, and if using, add a spoonful of rice.

-Top with lettuce, a dollop of sour cream, and a spoonful of guacamole.

3.Wrap the Burritos:

-Fold the sides of the tortilla over the filling, then roll it up from the bottom to the top, creating a secure burrito.

-For a more authentic look, you can wrap each burrito in foil to resemble the Battle Bus supply drops.

Battle Royale Burger

4 servings

Difficulty:

Easy

Claim victory with the ultimate Battle Royale Burger, inspired by the thrilling final battles of Fortnite. This towering burger combines juicy, seasoned beef patties with all the classic fixings, delivering a mouth-watering experience that's sure to satisfy any appetite. Perfect for game nights or a hearty meal with friends, this burger will keep you fueled for your next victory royale.

Ingredients:

For the Burger Patties:

- 1 pound (450 g) ground beef
- 1 teaspoon (5 g) salt
- 1/2 teaspoon (2.5 g) black pepper
- 1/2 teaspoon (2.5 g) garlic powder
- 1/2 teaspoon (2.5 g) onion powder

For the Special Sauce:

- 1/2 cup (120 ml) mayonnaise
- 2 tablespoons (30 ml) ketchup
- 1 tablespoon (15 ml) yellow mustard
- 1 tablespoon (15 ml) sweet pickle relish
- 1 teaspoon (5 ml) white vinegar
- 1/2 teaspoon (2.5 g) paprika
- 1/4 teaspoon (1.25 g) garlic powder
- 1/4 teaspoon (1.25 g) onion powder

For Assembling the Burgers:

- 4 hamburger buns
- 4 slices cheddar cheese
- Lettuce leaves
- Tomato slices
- Pickle slices
- Red onion slices

Instructions:

1.Prepare the Special Sauce:

-In a small bowl, combine the mayonnaise, ketchup, yellow mustard, sweet pickle relish, white vinegar, paprika, garlic powder, and onion powder. Mix well until all ingredients are thoroughly combined.

-Cover and refrigerate the sauce while you prepare the rest of the ingredients.

2.Prepare the Burger Patties:

-In a large bowl, combine the ground beef, salt, black pepper, garlic powder, and onion powder. Mix gently until just combined, being careful not to overwork the meat.

-Divide the mixture into four equal portions and shape each portion into a patty, about 1/2 inch (1.25 cm) thick. Make a small indentation in the center of each patty to prevent it from puffing up during cooking.

3.Cook the Burger Patties:

-Preheat a grill or skillet over medium-high heat. If using a skillet, add a small amount of oil to prevent sticking.

-Cook the patties for about 3-4 minutes on each side, or until they reach your desired level of doneness. In the last minute of cooking, place a slice of cheddar cheese on each patty and cover the grill or skillet to melt the cheese.

4.Toast the Buns:

-While the patties are cooking, lightly toast the hamburger buns on the grill or in a toaster until they are golden brown.

5.Assemble the Burgers and serve.

Cozy Campfire Chili

Warm up by the fire with Cozy Campfire Chili, inspired by the comforting and communal feel of Fortnite's cozy campfires. This hearty chili is packed with robust flavors, featuring tender beef, beans, and a blend of spices that create a rich and satisfying meal. Perfect for gatherings or a solo feast, this chili is sure to keep you cozy and ready for your next adventure.

Ingredients:

•2 tablespoons (30 ml) olive oil

•1 large onion, diced

•4 cloves garlic, minced

•1 pound (450 g) ground beef

•1 bell pepper, diced

•2 jalapeños, seeded and diced (optional for extra heat)

•2 tablespoons (30 g) chili powder

•1 tablespoon (15 g) ground cumin

•1 teaspoon (5 g) smoked paprika

•1/2 teaspoon (2.5 g) cayenne pepper

•1/2 teaspoon (2.5 g) black pepper

•1 can (15 ounces / 425 g) kidney beans, drained and rinsed

•1 can (15 ounces / 425 g) black beans, drained and rinsed

•1 can (15 ounces / 425 g) diced tomatoes

•1 can (15 ounces / 425 g) tomato sauce

•1 cup (240 ml) beef broth

•1 tablespoon Worcestershire sauce

•1 tablespoon (15 g) brown sugar

•1 cup (240 ml) corn kernels

•Juice of 1 lime

Instructions:

1.Prepare the Aromatics:

-In a large pot or Dutch oven, heat the olive oil over medium-high heat.

-Add the diced onion and sauté until it becomes translucent, about 5 minutes.

-Add the minced garlic and cook for an additional minute until fragrant.

2.Brown the Beef:

-Add the ground beef to the pot and cook until browned, breaking it apart with a spoon as it cooks, about 7-8 minutes.

-Drain any excess fat if necessary.

3.Add the Vegetables:

-Stir in the diced bell pepper and jalapeños (if using) and cook for another 3-4 minutes until they start to soften.

-Add the chili powder, ground cumin, smoked paprika, cayenne pepper (if using), salt, and black pepper. Stir well to coat the beef and vegetables

4.Add the Beans and Tomatoes:

-Stir in the kidney beans, black beans, diced tomatoes, tomato sauce, and beef broth.

-Add the Worcestershire sauce and brown sugar, and mix well to combine.

5.Simmer the Chili:

-Bring the mixture to a boil, then reduce the heat to low and let it simmer, uncovered, for about 30-45 minutes, stirring occasionally.

-Add the corn kernels during the last 10 minutes of cooking.

7.Finish with Lime and Cilantro:

Craggy Cliffs Clam Chowder

4-6 servings
Difficulty:
Medium

This creamy, hearty chowder is brimming with tender clams, potatoes, and a blend of savory herbs, making it the perfect dish to warm you up after a long day of adventures. Rich and comforting, this clam chowder is a culinary treasure that brings a taste of the sea to your table.

Ingredients:

- 4 slices bacon, chopped
- 1 large onion, finely chopped
- 2 cloves garlic, minced
- 3 stalks celery, finely chopped
- 2 large potatoes, peeled and diced
- 2 cans (10 ounces / 283 g each) clams, with juice
- 1 bottle (8 ounces / 240 ml) clam juice
- 1 cup (240 ml) heavy cream
- 2 cups (480 ml) whole milk
- 1 cup (240 ml) chicken broth
- 1 teaspoon (5 g) dried thyme
- 1 teaspoon (5 g) dried dill
- 1 bay leaf
- Salt and pepper to taste
- Fresh parsley, chopped (for garnish)
- Oyster crackers (for serving)

Instructions:

1.Cook the Bacon:

-In a large pot or Dutch oven, cook the chopped bacon over medium heat until crispy. Remove the bacon with a slotted spoon and set aside, leaving the rendered fat in the pot.

2.Sauté the Vegetables:

-Add the finely chopped onion, minced garlic, and finely chopped celery to the pot with the bacon fat. Sauté until the vegetables are soft and translucent, about 5-7 minutes.

3.Add the Potatoes and Liquids:

-Stir in the diced potatoes, clam juice from the cans, bottled clam juice, chicken broth, and dried thyme, dried dill, and bay leaf.

-Bring the mixture to a boil, then reduce the heat and let it simmer for about 15-20 minutes, or until the potatoes are tender.

4.Add the Clams and Dairy:

-Stir in the clams, heavy cream, and whole milk. Let the chowder simmer for an additional 5-10 minutes, allowing the flavors to meld together. Do not let it boil.

5.Season and Serve:

-Remove the bay leaf and season the chowder with salt and pepper to taste.

-Ladle the clam chowder into bowls and garnish with the crispy bacon and chopped fresh parsley.

-Serve with oyster crackers on the side.

Cuddle Team Leader's Curry

This vibrant and flavorful curry combines tender chicken, a blend of aromatic spices, and creamy coconut milk, creating a dish that's as heartwarming as a hug from the Cuddle Team Leader. Perfect for a cozy dinner, this curry will bring joy and comfort to your table with every delicious bite.

Ingredients:

- 2 tablespoons (30 ml) vegetable oil
- 1 large onion, finely chopped
- 3 cloves garlic, minced
- 1 tablespoon (15 g) fresh ginger, minced
- 1 pound (450 g) boneless, skinless chicken breasts or thighs, cut into bite-sized pieces
- 2 tablespoons (30 g) curry powder
- 1 teaspoon (5 g) ground cumin
- 1 teaspoon (5 g) ground coriander
- 1/2 teaspoon (2.5 g) turmeric
- 1/2 teaspoon (2.5 g) cayenne pepper (optional, for extra heat)
- 1 can (14.5 ounces / 410 g) tomatoes
- 1 can (14 ounces / 400 ml) coconut milk
- 1 cup (240 ml) chicken broth
- 1/4 cup (60 ml) fresh cilantro, chopped (for garnish)
- Juice of 1 lime (optional, for garnish)
- 2 cups (400 g) basmati or jasmine rice

Instructions:

1.Prepare the Rice:

-Rinse the rice under cold water until the water runs clear.

-In a medium saucepan, bring the water to a boil. Add the salt and rice.

-Reduce the heat to low, cover, and simmer for 15-20 minutes, or until the rice is cooked and the water is absorbed.

-Fluff the rice with a fork and keep warm.

2.Prepare the Chicken Curry:

-In a large skillet or Dutch oven, heat the vegetable oil over medium-high heat.

-Add the finely chopped onion and sauté until it becomes translucent, about 5 minutes.

-Add the minced garlic and ginger, and cook for another minute until fragrant.

-Add the chicken pieces to the skillet and cook until browned on all sides, about 5-7 minutes.

-Stir in the curry powder, ground cumin, ground coriander, turmeric, and cayenne pepper (if using). Cook for 1-2 minutes until the spices are fragrant.

-Add the diced tomatoes (with their juice), coconut milk, and chicken broth. Stir well to combine.

-Bring the mixture to a simmer, then reduce the heat to low. Cover and cook for 20-25 minutes, or until the chicken is cooked through and the sauce has thickened. Season with salt and pepper to taste.

3.Serve.

DC Ratatouille

4-6 servings

Difficulty:

Medium

This classic French dish features a medley of fresh, vibrant vegetables like zucchini, eggplant, bell peppers, and tomatoes, all slow-cooked to perfection. Bursting with rich, savory flavors and a touch of Provençal herbs, this ratatouille is a delightful and wholesome meal that brings a touch of elegance to your gaming sessions.

Ingredients:

For the Vegetables:

- 2 medium eggplants, cut into 1/2-inch (1.3 cm) cubes
- 2 medium zucchinis, sliced into 1/4-inch (0.6 cm) rounds
- 1 large yellow bell pepper, cut into 1/2-inch (1.3 cm) pieces
- 1 large red bell pepper, cut into 1/2-inch (1.3 cm) pieces
- 1 large onion, finely chopped
- 4 cloves garlic, minced
- 4 medium tomatoes, chopped
- 1/4 cup (60 ml) olive oil
- Salt and pepper to taste

For the Seasoning:

- 1 teaspoon (5 g) dried thyme
- 1 teaspoon (5 g) dried oregano
- 1/2 teaspoon (2.5 g) dried basil
- 1/2 teaspoon (2.5 g) dried rosemary
- 2 bay leaves
- 1/4 cup (60 ml) fresh basil, chopped (for garnish)

Instructions:

1.Prepare the Vegetables:

-Preheat your oven to 400°F (200°C).

-In a large bowl, toss the eggplant cubes with a little salt. Let them sit for about 15 minutes to draw out excess moisture. Rinse and pat dry with paper towels.

-In a large roasting pan or baking sheet, combine the eggplant, zucchini, yellow bell pepper, red bell pepper, and onion.

-Drizzle the vegetables with olive oil and season with salt and pepper. Toss to coat evenly.

-Spread the vegetables in a single layer on the roasting pan.

2.Roast the Vegetables:

-Roast in the preheated oven for about 30-35 minutes, stirring halfway through, until the vegetables are tender and lightly browned.

3.Prepare the Ratatouille:

-In a large, heavy-bottomed pot or Dutch oven, heat a bit more olive oil over medium heat.

-Add the minced garlic and sauté for about 1 minute until fragrant.

-Add the chopped tomatoes and cook for about 5-7 minutes until they begin to break down and release their juices.

-Stir in the roasted vegetables, dried thyme, dried oregano, dried basil, dried rosemary, and bay leaves.

-Reduce the heat to low and let the ratatouille simmer for about 20-25 minutes, stirring occasionally, until the flavors are well combined.

4.Serve.

Epic Eggplant Parmesan

This dish features thick slices of eggplant, expertly breaded and fried until crispy, then layered with rich marinara sauce and gooey mozzarella cheese. Baked to a bubbling, golden perfection, this epic creation delivers a mouthwatering combination of flavors and textures that will elevate any mealtime. Perfect for a hearty feast, this eggplant parmesan is a game-changer in your culinary arsenal.

Ingredients:

- 2 large eggplants
- 1 tablespoon (15 g) salt
- 1 cup (120 g) all-purpose flour
- 3 large eggs, beaten
- 2 cups (240 g) breadcrumbs
- 1/2 cup (50 g) grated Parmesan cheese
- 1 teaspoon (5 g) dried oregano
- 1 teaspoon (5 g) dried basil
- 1/2 teaspoon (2.5 g) garlic powder
- 1/2 teaspoon (2.5 g) black pepper
- 1/4 cup (60 ml) olive oil

For the Marinara Sauce:

- 2 tablespoons (30 ml) olive oil
- 1 small onion, finely chopped
- 3 cloves garlic, minced
- 1 can (28 ounces / 800 g) crushed tomatoes
- 1 teaspoon (5 g) dried oregano
- 1 teaspoon (5 g) dried basil
- 1/2 teaspoon (2.5 g) red pepper flakes (optional)
- 1/4 cup (60 ml) chopped fresh basil
- 2 cups (200 g) shredded mozzarella cheese

Instructions

-Slice the eggplants into 1/4-inch (0.6 cm) thick rounds.

-Lay the slices on a baking sheet and sprinkle both sides generously with salt. Let them sit for 30 minutes to draw out excess moisture

-After 30 minutes, rinse the eggplant slices under cold water and dry

-Set up a breading station with three shallow bowls: one with flour, one with beaten eggs, and one with breadcrumbs mixed with 1/2 cup (50 g) grated Parmesan, dried oregano, dried basil, garlic powder

-Dredge each eggplant slice in the flour, shaking off any excess, then dip it in the beaten eggs, and finally coat it with the breadcrumb mixture

-Arrange the breaded eggplant slices on a baking sheet

-Drizzle the slices with olive oil or use an oil spray to lightly coat them.

-Bake in the preheated oven for 20-25 minutes, flipping halfway

-While the eggplant is baking, heat 2 tablespoons (30 ml) of olive oil

-Add the finely chopped onion and sauté until translucen

-Add the minced garlic and cook for another minute until fragrant.

-Stir in the crushed tomatoes, dried oregano, dried basil and season

-Simmer the sauce for 15-20 minutes, stirring occasionally.

-In a large baking dish, spread a thin layer of marinara sauce

-Arrange a layer of baked eggplant slices over the sauce.

-Spoon more marinara sauce over the eggplant, and sprinkle with shredded mozzarella and grated Parmesan.

-Repeat the layers until all the eggplant slices are used, finishing with a layer of sauce and cheese.

-Cover the baking dish with foil and bake in the preheated oven for 20 minutes.

-Remove the foil and bake for an additional 15-20 minutes and serve

Fatal Fields Frittata

Harvest a bounty of flavors with the Fatal Fields Frittata, inspired by the fertile lands of Fortnite's Fatal Fields. This hearty and wholesome dish combines fresh vegetables, savory cheese, and fluffy eggs to create a perfect frittata that's both satisfying and nutritious. Ideal for breakfast, brunch, or a quick dinner, this frittata captures the essence of farm-fresh goodness, bringing the rustic charm of Fatal Fields right to your table.

Ingredients:

For the Frittata:

- 8 large eggs
- 1/4 cup (60 ml) milk (whole or 2%)
- 1 cup (100 g) shredded cheddar cheese
- 1/2 cup (50 g) grated Parmesan cheese
- 1 tablespoon (15 ml) olive oil
- 1 small onion, finely chopped
- 1 red bell pepper, diced
- 1 zucchini, diced
- 1 cup (150 g) cherry tomatoes, halved
- 2 cups (60 g) fresh spinach, chopped
- 2 cloves garlic, minced
- 1 teaspoon (5 g) dried oregano
- 1/2 teaspoon (2.5 g) salt
- 1/2 teaspoon (2.5 g) black pepper
- Fresh herbs for garnish (such as parsley, basil, or chives)

Instructions:

1.Preheat the Oven:

-Preheat your oven to 375°F (190°C).

2.Prepare the Egg Mixture:

-In a large bowl, whisk together the eggs and milk until well combined.

-Stir in the shredded cheddar cheese and grated Parmesan cheese. Set aside.

3.Cook the Vegetables:

-In an oven-safe skillet (such as a cast-iron skillet), heat the olive oil over medium heat.

-Add the finely chopped onion and cook until it becomes translucent, about 5 minutes.

-Add the diced red bell pepper, zucchini, and minced garlic. Cook for another 5 minutes until the vegetables are softened.

-Stir in the halved cherry tomatoes and chopped spinach. Cook until the spinach is wilted, about 2 minutes.

-Sprinkle the dried oregano, salt, and black pepper over the vegetables. Mix well.

4.Combine and Cook:

-Pour the egg mixture over the cooked vegetables in the skillet. Stir gently to distribute the vegetables evenly.

-Cook on the stovetop over medium heat for about 3-4 minutes, until the edges start to set.

-Transfer the skillet to the preheated oven and bake for 15-20 minutes, or until the frittata is fully set and the top is golden brown.

-A toothpick inserted into the center should come out clean

6.Serve.

Flare BBQ Sandwiches

Ignite your taste buds with Flare BBQ Sandwiches, inspired by the fiery excitement of Fortnite's flare guns. These sandwiches feature tender, slow-cooked pulled pork drenched in a smoky and tangy BBQ sauce, piled high on a toasted bun. Topped with crunchy coleslaw for an added burst of flavor and texture, each bite delivers a perfect balance of heat and sweetness. Perfect for a cookout or a game night feast, these BBQ sandwiches are sure to light up any occasion.

Ingredients:

For the Pulled Pork:

- 3-4 pounds (1.4-1.8 kg) pork shoulder or pork butt
- 1 tablespoon (15 g) brown sugar
- 1 tablespoon (15 g) paprika
- 1 teaspoon (5 g) garlic powder
- 1 teaspoon (5 g) onion powder
- 1 teaspoon (5 g) ground cumin
- 1 teaspoon (5 g) salt
- 1/2 teaspoon (2.5 g) black pepper
- 1/2 teaspoon (2.5 g) cayenne pepper (optional, for extra heat)
- 1 cup (240 ml) BBQ sauce
- 1/2 cup (120 ml) apple cider vinegar
- 1/2 cup (120 ml) chicken broth

For the Sandwiches:

- 8 hamburger buns or soft rolls
- Coleslaw (optional, for topping)
- Extra BBQ sauce (for serving)
- Pickles (optional, for serving)

Instructions:

1.Prepare the Pork:

-In a small bowl, mix together the brown sugar, paprika, garlic powder, onion powder, ground cumin, salt, black pepper, and cayenne pepper (if using).

-Rub the spice mixture all over the pork shoulder, ensuring it is evenly coated.

2.Slow Cook the Pork:

-Place the seasoned pork shoulder in a slow cooker.

-Pour the BBQ sauce, apple cider vinegar, and chicken broth over the pork.

-Cover and cook on low for 8-10 hours or on high for 4-6 hours, until the pork is tender and easily shreds with a fork.

3.Shred the Pork:

-Once the pork is cooked, remove it from the slow cooker and place it on a large cutting board.

-Use two forks to shred the pork into bite-sized pieces.

-Return the shredded pork to the slow cooker and mix it with the cooking juices to keep it moist and flavorful.

4.Prepare the Sandwiches:

-Toast the hamburger buns or soft rolls if desired.

-Pile the pulled pork onto the bottom half of each bun.

-Top with coleslaw if using, and drizzle with extra BBQ sauce.

5.Serve.

Frosty Flights Fish & Chips

Soar into a classic British favorite with Frosty Flights Fish & Chips, inspired by the icy adventures of Fortnite's Frosty Flights. This dish features flaky white fish coated in a crispy, golden batter, served alongside thick-cut, perfectly fried chips. Accompanied by tangy tartar sauce and a splash of malt vinegar, this fish and chips combo brings a taste of seaside comfort to your table. Ideal for a cozy dinner or a fun gathering, this meal is sure to be a hit with everyone.

Ingredients:

For the Fish:

- 1 1/2 pounds (680 g) white fish fillets (such as cod or haddock)
- 1 cup (120 g) all-purpose flour
- 1 teaspoon (5 g) baking powder
- 1/2 teaspoon (2.5 g) salt
- 1/4 teaspoon (1.25 g) black pepper
- 1 cup (240 ml) cold sparkling water or beer
- Extra flour for dredging
- Vegetable oil for frying

For the Chips:

- 4 large russet potatoes, peeled and cut into thick fries
- 2 tablespoons (30 ml) vegetable oil
- Salt to taste

For Serving:

- Malt vinegar
- Lemon wedges
- Tartar sauce

Instructions:

1.Prepare the Chips:

-Preheat your oven to 425°F (220°C).

-Rinse the cut potatoes in cold water and pat them dry with a clean kitchen towel.

-Toss the potato fries with vegetable oil and spread them in a single layer on a baking sheet.

-Bake in the preheated oven for 25-30 minutes, flipping halfway through, until golden brown and crispy.

-Season with salt to taste and keep warm.

2.Prepare the Fish Batter:

-In a large bowl, whisk together the flour, baking powder, salt, and black pepper.

-Gradually add the cold sparkling water or beer, whisking until the batter is smooth and free of lumps.

3.Dredge and Fry the Fish:

-Heat vegetable oil in a deep frying pan or pot to 350°F (175°C). The oil should be about 2-3 inches (5-7 cm) deep.

-Pat the fish fillets dry with paper towels and lightly dredge them in flour, shaking off any excess.

-Dip the dredged fish fillets into the batter, allowing any excess to drip

-Carefully lower the battered fish into the hot oil and fry in batches for 4-5 minutes per side, or until golden brown and crispy.

-Remove the fried fish with a slotted spoon and drain on paper towels.

4.Serve.

Greasy Grove Gyros

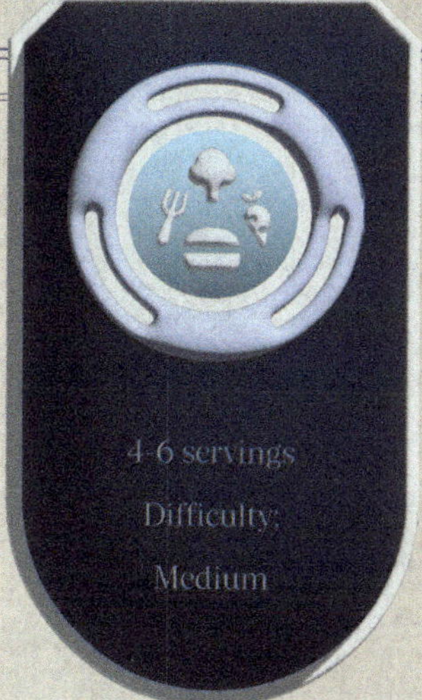

These gyros feature succulent slices of marinated lamb or chicken, wrapped in warm pita bread and topped with fresh veggies, tangy tzatziki sauce, and a sprinkle of feta cheese. Each bite is a delightful combination of savory, creamy, and crunchy textures, making it a perfect meal for any time of day. Whether you're refueling after a game or enjoying a relaxed meal, these gyros bring the taste of Greasy Grove straight to your kitchen.

Ingredients:

- 1 pound (450 g) ground lamb
- 1 small onion, finely grated
- 3 cloves garlic, minced
- 1 teaspoon (5 g) dried oregano
- 1 teaspoon (5 g) ground cumin
- 1 teaspoon (5 g) ground coriander
- 1/2 teaspoon (2.5 g) ground cinnamon
- 1/2 teaspoon (2.5 g) salt
- 1/2 teaspoon (2.5 g) black pepper
- 1 tablespoon (15 ml) olive oil
- 1 cup (240 ml) Greek yogurt
- 1/2 cucumber, grated and excess water squeezed out
- 1 tablespoon (15 ml) lemon juice
- 1 tablespoon (15 ml) olive oil
- 2 cloves garlic, minced
- 1 tablespoon (15 g) fresh dill, chopped
- 4-6 pita breads
- 1 cup (150 g) cherry tomatoes, halved
- 1 small red onion, thinly sliced
- 1 cup (150 g) shredded lettuce
- 1/2 cup (75 g) crumbled feta cheese
- Fresh parsley or mint leaves for garnish

Instructions:

1.Prepare the Lamb:

-In a large bowl, combine the ground lamb, grated onion, minced garlic, dried oregano, ground cumin, ground coriander, ground cinnamon, salt, and black pepper. Mix well until all the ingredients are evenly incorporated.

-Heat the olive oil in a large skillet over medium-high heat.

-Add the lamb mixture to the skillet and cook, breaking it up with a spoon, until browned and fully cooked, about 8-10 minutes. Drain any excess fat if necessary.

2.Prepare the Tzatziki Sauce:

-In a bowl, combine the Greek yogurt, grated cucumber, lemon juice, olive oil, minced garlic, and chopped fresh dill. Mix well.

-Season with salt and pepper to taste. Refrigerate until ready to use.

3.Warm the Pita Breads:

-While the lamb is cooking, warm the pita breads in a dry skillet over medium heat, or wrap them in a damp paper towel and microwave for about 30 seconds to make them pliable.

-Spread a generous amount of tzatziki sauce inside each warm pita bread.

-Add a portion of the cooked lamb mixture.

-Top with cherry tomatoes, thinly sliced red onion, shredded lettuce, and crumbled feta cheese.

Garnish with fresh parsley or mint leaves.

4.Serve.

Greazy Sloppy Joes

These very sloppy sandwiches feature ground beef simmered in a rich, tangy tomato sauce, seasoned to perfection and served on soft, toasted buns. Each bite is a satisfying explosion of flavors and textures, perfect for satisfying your hunger during an intense gaming session or a casual meal with friends. Easy to make and impossible to resist.

Ingredients:

- 1 pound (450 g) ground beef
- 1 small onion, finely chopped
- 1 small green bell pepper, finely chopped
- 2 cloves garlic, minced
- 1 cup (240 ml) tomato sauce
- 1/4 cup (60 ml) ketchup
- 2 tablespoons (30 ml) Worcestershire sauce
- 1 tablespoon (15 ml) brown sugar
- 1 teaspoon (5 ml) yellow mustard
- Salt and pepper to taste
- 4 hamburger buns

Instructions:

1.Cook the Ground Beef:

-In a large skillet, cook the ground beef over medium heat until browned. Drain any excess fat.

2.Sauté the Vegetables:

-Add the finely chopped onion and green bell pepper to the skillet with the ground beef. Cook until the vegetables are softened, about 5 minutes.

-Add the minced garlic and cook for another minute until fragrant.

3.Add the Sauce Ingredients:

-Stir in the tomato sauce, ketchup, Worcestershire sauce, brown sugar, and yellow mustard.

-Season with salt and pepper to taste.

4.Simmer the Mixture:

-Reduce the heat to low and let the mixture simmer for about 10-15 minutes, stirring occasionally, until the sauce is thickened and the flavors are well combined.

5.Toast the Buns (optional):

-If desired, lightly toast the hamburger buns in a separate skillet or toaster.

6.Assemble the Sloppy Joes:

-Spoon the meat mixture onto the bottom halves of the hamburger buns.

-Place the top halves of the buns on top and serve immediately.

Happy Hamlet Hotdogs

Bring the festive spirit of Happy Hamlet to your table with these delicious hotdogs. Inspired by the joyful ambiance of Fortnite's charming village, these hotdogs feature juicy, grilled sausages nestled in warm buns and topped with a delightful array of toppings like tangy sauerkraut, crispy onions, and creamy mustard. Perfect for a quick lunch, a game night snack, or a backyard barbecue, these hotdogs will add a touch of happiness to any meal. Enjoy the simple yet satisfying flavors that are sure to make your taste buds dance with delight.

Ingredients:

•8 high-quality beef sausages

•8 hotdog buns

•Butter or olive oil for toasting the buns

Toppings:

Classic New York Style:

•Sauerkraut

•Spicy brown mustard

•Onion sauce (optional)

Chicago Style:

•Yellow mustard

•Sweet pickle relish

•Chopped onions

•Tomato slices

•Pickle spears

•Sport peppers

•Celery salt

Southern Style:

•Coleslaw

•BBQ sauce

•Chopped onions

Tex-Mex Style:

•Guacamole

•Pico de gallo

•Jalapeño slices

•Shredded cheese

Instructions:

1.Prepare the Hotdogs:

-Grill or cook the hotdogs according to the package instructions. For an added layer of flavor, you can also pan-fry them until they are nicely browned.

2.Toast the Buns:

-Lightly butter or brush the insides of the hotdog buns with olive oil.

-Toast them on the grill or in a skillet until they are golden brown.

3.Assemble the Hotdogs:

-Place each hotdog in a toasted bun.

-Add your desired toppings from the different styles listed above. You can mix and match or stick to one theme.

4.Serve:

-Arrange the hotdogs on a serving platter.

-Provide additional condiments and toppings on the side for guests to customize their hotdogs.

Weeping Woods Waffles and Chicken

This dish features crispy, golden fried chicken paired with fluffy, homemade waffles, creating a delightful balance of savory and sweet. Drizzled with warm maple syrup and a sprinkle of fresh herbs, each bite is a perfect harmony of textures and tastes. Ideal for a hearty breakfast, brunch, or dinner, this combination brings the rustic charm and tranquility of Weeping Woods to your plate. Enjoy this comforting meal that's sure to satisfy and delight.

4 servings
Difficulty:
Medium

Ingredients:

For the Fried Chicken:

- 1 pound (450 g) boneless, skinless chicken thighs or breasts
- 1 cup (240 ml) buttermilk
- 1 teaspoon (5 g) hot sauce (optional)
- 1 cup (120 g) all-purpose flour
- 1/2 cup (60 g) cornstarch
- 1 teaspoon (5 g) garlic powder
- 1 teaspoon (5 g) onion powder
- 1 teaspoon (5 g) smoked paprika
- 1/2 teaspoon (2.5 g) cayenne pepper
- Vegetable oil for frying

For the Waffles:

- 2 cups (240 g) all-purpose flour
- 2 tablespoons (25 g) granulated sugar
- 1 tablespoon (15 g) baking powder
- 1/2 teaspoon (2.5 g) salt
- 2 large eggs
- 1 3/4 cups (420 ml) milk
- 1/2 cup (115 g) unsalted butter
- 1 teaspoon (5 ml) vanilla extract

For Serving:

- Maple syrup
- Hot sauce (optional)

Instructions:

-In a large bowl, combine the buttermilk and hot sauce (if using).

-Add the chicken thighs or breasts to the bowl, ensuring they are fully submerged. Cover and refrigerate for at least 1 hour, or overnight

-In a shallow dish, whisk together the flour, cornstarch, garlic powder, onion powder, smoked paprika, cayenne pepper (if using), salt

-Heat about 1-2 inches (2.5-5 cm) of vegetable oil in a large skillet or deep frying pan over medium-high heat until it reaches 350°F (175°C).

-Dredge each piece of chicken in the flour mixture

-Fry the chicken in batches, turning occasionally, until golden brown and cooked through, about 6-8 minutes per side.

-Transfer the fried chicken to a paper towel-lined plate

-In a large bowl, whisk together the flour, granulated sugar, baking powder, and salt.

-In a separate bowl, beat the eggs and then whisk in the milk, melted butter, and vanilla extract.

-Pour the wet ingredients into the dry ingredients and stir until just combined. Do not overmix; some lumps are okay.

-Preheat your waffle iron according to the manufacturer's instructions.

-Lightly grease the waffle iron with cooking spray or melted butter.

-Pour the batter onto the hot waffle iron, using about 1/2 to 3/4 cup (120-180 ml) of batter per waffle, depending on the size of your waffle iron.

-Cook the waffles until golden brown and crisp, about 4-5 minutes. Repeat with the remaining batter.

6.Serve:

-Place a waffle on a plate, top with a piece of fried chicken, and drizzle with maple syrup. Add a pat of butter on top if desired.

High Ground Mac 'n Cheese

Elevate your culinary game with High Ground Mac 'n Cheese, inspired by the strategic advantage of Fortnite's high ground. This ultimate comfort food features tender pasta enveloped in a rich and creamy cheese sauce, topped with a crispy breadcrumb crust for added texture. Bursting with cheesy goodness, each bite delivers a satisfying combination of flavors that will keep you coming back for more. Perfect for a cozy dinner or a hearty side dish, this mac 'n cheese is sure to become a favorite in your culinary arsenal.

Ingredients:

For the Macaroni:

- 1 pound (450 g) elbow macaroni or pasta of your choice

For the Cheese Sauce:

- 4 tablespoons (60 g) unsalted butter
- 1/4 cup (30 g) all-purpose flour
- 4 cups (960 ml) whole milk
- 1 cup (240 ml) heavy cream
- 2 teaspoons (10 g) Dijon mustard
- 1 teaspoon (5 g) garlic powder
- 1/2 teaspoon (2.5 g) onion powder
- 1/2 teaspoon (2.5 g) smoked paprika
- 2 cups (200 g) shredded sharp cheddar cheese
- 1 cup (100 g) shredded Gruyère cheese
- 1 cup (100 g) shredded Parmesan cheese
- Salt and black pepper to taste

For the Topping:

- 1 cup (100 g) panko breadcrumbs
- 2 tablespoons (30 g) unsalted butter, melted
- 1/4 cup (25 g) grated Parmesan cheese
- 1 tablespoon (15 g) fresh parsley.

Instructions:

1.Cook the Macaroni:

-Bring a large pot of salted water to a boil.

-Add the macaroni and cook according to the package instructions

-Drain and set aside.

2.Prepare the Cheese Sauce:

-In a large saucepan, melt the butter over medium heat.

-Stir in the flour and cook for 2-3 minutes, stirring constantly

-Gradually whisk in the milk and heavy cream, continuing to stir until the mixture is smooth and begins to thicken, about 5-7 minutes.

-Add the Dijon mustard, garlic powder, onion powder, and smoked paprika. Stir to combine.

-Reduce the heat to low and gradually add the shredded cheddar, Gruyère, and Parmesan cheeses, stirring until completely melted

-Season the sauce with salt and black pepper to taste.

3.Combine the Macaroni and Cheese Sauce:

-Preheat your oven to 375°F (190°C).

-Add the cooked macaroni to the cheese sauce, stirring gently to combine until the pasta is evenly coated.

-In a small bowl, mix the panko breadcrumbs with the melted butter until the breadcrumbs are evenly coated.

-Stir in the grated Parmesan cheese and chopped fresh parsley if using.

4.Assemble and Bake:

-Transfer the macaroni and cheese mixture to a greased baking dish.

-Evenly sprinkle the breadcrumb topping over the macaroni and cheese.

-Bake in the preheated oven for 20-25 minutes, or until the topping is golden brown and the cheese sauce is bubbly and serve.

Junk Junction Jambalaya

Embark on a flavor-packed adventure with Junk Junction Jambalaya, inspired by the eclectic and industrious vibe of Fortnite's Junk Junction. This vibrant dish combines tender chicken, succulent shrimp, and spicy sausage with a medley of rice, tomatoes, and aromatic Cajun spices. Each spoonful offers a rich and satisfying burst of flavor that transports you straight to the heart of Louisiana. Perfect for a hearty dinner or a festive gathering, this jambalaya brings a taste of the bayou to your table, making every meal an exciting culinary journey.

Ingredients:

For the Jambalaya:

- 1 pound (450 g) large shrimp, peeled and deveined
- 2 tablespoons (30 ml) olive oil
- 1 pound (450 g) andouille sausage, sliced
- 1 large onion, diced
- 1 green bell pepper, diced
- 1 red bell pepper, diced
- 2 celery stalks, diced
- 4 cloves garlic, minced
- 1 cup (200 g) long-grain rice
- 1 can (14.5 ounces / 410 g) diced tomatoes
- 4 cups (1 liter) chicken broth
- 2 teaspoons (10 g) smoked paprika
- 1 teaspoon (5 g) dried thyme
- 1 teaspoon (5 g) dried oregano
- 1 teaspoon (5 g) cayenne pepper (adjust to taste)
- 2 bay leaves
- Salt and pepper to taste
- 1/4 cup (60 ml) fresh parsley, chopped
- 4 green onions, sliced

Instructions:

1.Cook the Macaroni:

-Bring a large pot of salted water to a boil.

-Add the macaroni and cook according to the package instructions

-Drain and set aside.

2.Prepare the Cheese Sauce:

-In a large saucepan, melt the butter over medium heat.

-Stir in the flour and cook for 2-3 minutes, stirring constantly

-Gradually whisk in the milk and heavy cream, continuing to stir until the mixture is smooth and begins to thicken, about 5-7 minutes.

-Add the Dijon mustard, garlic powder, onion powder, and smoked paprika. Stir to combine.

-Reduce the heat to low and gradually add the shredded cheddar, Gruyère, and Parmesan cheeses, stirring until completely melted

-Season the sauce with salt and black pepper to taste.

3.Combine the Macaroni and Cheese Sauce:

-Preheat your oven to 375°F (190°C).

-Add the cooked macaroni to the cheese sauce, stirring gently to combine until the pasta is evenly coated.

-In a small bowl, mix the panko breadcrumbs with the melted butter until the breadcrumbs are evenly coated.

-Stir in the grated Parmesan cheese and chopped fresh parsley if using.

4.Assemble and Bake:

-Transfer the macaroni and cheese mixture to a greased baking dish.

-Evenly sprinkle the breadcrumb topping over the macaroni and cheese.

-Bake in the preheated oven for 20-25 minutes, or until the topping is golden brown and the cheese sauce is bubbly and serve.

Layers and Layers of Lasagna

This classic Italian dish features multiple layers of tender pasta sheets, rich meat sauce, creamy ricotta, and gooey mozzarella cheese, all baked to golden perfection. Each layer adds a new depth of flavor, making every bite a delicious journey through savory goodness. Perfect for family dinners or special occasions, this lasagna is a comforting and satisfying meal that brings a touch of culinary craftsmanship to your table.

Ingredients:

•1 pound (450 g) ground beef
•1 tablespoon (15 ml) olive oil
•1 large onion, finely chopped
•4 cloves garlic, minced
•1 can (28 ounces / 800 g) tomatoes
•1 can (6 ounces / 170 g) tomato paste
•1 can (15 ounces / 425 g) tomato sauce
•1/2 cup (120 ml) red wine (optional)
•2 teaspoons (10 g) sugar
•2 teaspoons (10 g) dried basil
•1 teaspoon (5 g) dried oregano
•1/2 teaspoon (2.5 g) salt
•1/4 teaspoon (1.25 g) black pepper
•1/4 teaspoon (1.25 g) red pepper flakes
•1/4 cup (60 ml) fresh parsley, chopped
•15 ounces (425 g) ricotta cheese
•1 egg
•1/4 cup (25 g) grated Parmesan cheese
•2 tablespoons (30 ml) fresh parsley,
•12 lasagna noodles
•1 pound (450 g) mozzarella cheese, shredded
•1/2 cup (50 g) grated Parmesan cheese

Instructions:

-In a large skillet or Dutch oven, heat the olive oil over medium-high
-Add the finely chopped onion and sauté until translucent
-Add the minced garlic and cook for another minute until fragrant.
-Add the ground beef to the skillet and cook until browned, breaking it up with a spoon as it cooks. Drain any excess fat.
-Stir in the crushed tomatoes, tomato paste, tomato sauce
-Add the sugar, dried basil, dried oregano, salt, black pepper, and red pepper flakes (if using). Stir well to combine.
-Bring the sauce to a simmer and let it cook for 30 minutes, stirring occasionally. Stir in the chopped fresh parsley at the end.
-In a medium bowl, combine the ricotta cheese, egg, grated Parmesan cheese, and chopped fresh parsley. Mix well and set aside.
-While the meat sauce is simmering, cook the lasagna noodles according to the package instructions. Drain and set aside.
-Spread a thin layer of meat sauce on the bottom of a baking dish
-Place a layer of cooked lasagna noodles over the sauce.
-Spread a layer of the ricotta cheese mixture over the noodles.
-Sprinkle a layer of shredded mozzarella cheese over the ricotta mixture.
-Repeat the layers (meat sauce, noodles, ricotta mixture, mozzarella cheese) until you run out of ingredients, ending with a layer of meat sauce and a generous topping of shredded mozzarella
-Cover the baking dish with aluminum foil (to prevent sticking, you can spray the foil with a little cooking spray).
-Bake in the preheated oven for 25 minutes.
-Remove the foil and bake for an additional 25 minutes, or until the lasagna is bubbly and the cheese is golden brown and serve.

Loot Lake Salmon

Savor the fresh and vibrant flavors of Loot Lake Salmon, inspired by the serene and picturesque waters of Fortnite's Loot Lake. This dish features perfectly seared salmon fillets, seasoned with a blend of herbs and spices, and served with a zesty lemon butter sauce. Accompanied by a medley of fresh vegetables or a light salad, each bite of this succulent salmon brings a taste of tranquility and elegance to your meal. Ideal for a healthy dinner or a special occasion, Loot Lake Salmon is a delightful way to enjoy the bounty of the lake.

Ingredients:

For the Grilled Salmon:

- 4 salmon fillets (about 6 ounces / 170 g each)
- 2 tablespoons (30 ml) olive oil
- Salt and pepper to taste
- 1 lemon, thinly sliced

For the Lemon-Dill Sauce:

- 1/2 cup (120 ml) Greek yogurt
- 2 tablespoons (30 ml) mayonnaise
- 2 tablespoons (30 ml) fresh lemon juice
- 1 teaspoon (5 g) lemon zest
- 2 tablespoons (30 g) fresh dill, finely chopped
- 1 clove garlic, minced
- Salt and pepper to taste

For Garnish:

- Fresh dill sprigs
- Lemon wedges

Instructions:

1.Prepare the Salmon:

-Preheat your grill to medium-high heat.

-Brush the salmon fillets with olive oil and season generously with salt and pepper.

-Place lemon slices on top of each fillet.

2.Grill the Salmon:

-Lightly oil the grill grates to prevent sticking.

-Place the salmon fillets on the grill, skin-side down if the skin is on.

-Grill for about 4-5 minutes per side, or until the salmon is opaque and flakes easily with a fork. Cooking time may vary depending on the thickness of the fillets.

3.Prepare the Lemon-Dill Sauce:

-In a small bowl, combine the Greek yogurt, mayonnaise, fresh lemon juice, lemon zest, chopped dill, and minced garlic.

-Mix well until smooth and creamy.

-Season with salt and pepper to taste. Adjust the lemon juice and dill according to your preference.

4.Serve:

-Place the grilled salmon fillets on serving plates.

-Spoon a generous amount of the lemon-dill sauce over each fillet.

-Garnish with fresh dill sprigs and lemon wedges.

Mega Mall Meatballs

Experience the ultimate culinary shopping spree with Mega Mall Meatballs, inspired by the bustling and vibrant energy of Fortnite's Mega Mall. These savory meatballs are made from a blend of ground beef and pork, seasoned with a mix of Italian herbs and spices, and simmered in a rich marinara sauce. Perfectly tender and bursting with flavor, they can be served over pasta, in a sub sandwich, or as a delicious appetizer.

4-6 servings
Difficulty:
Medium

Ingredients:

For the Meatballs:

- 1 pound (450 g) ground beef
- 1/2 pound (225 g) ground pork
- 1/2 cup (50 g) breadcrumbs
- 1/4 cup (25 g) grated Parmesan cheese
- 2 cloves garlic, minced
- 1/4 cup (60 ml) milk
- 1 large egg
- 2 tablespoons (30 ml) fresh parsley, chopped
- 1 teaspoon (5 g) dried oregano
- 1/2 teaspoon (2.5 g) red pepper flakes

For the Marinara Sauce:

- 2 tablespoons (30 ml) olive oil
- 1 small onion, finely chopped
- 3 cloves garlic, minced
- 1 can (28 ounces / 800 g) tomatoes
- 1 teaspoon (5 g) dried oregano
- 1 teaspoon (5 g) dried basil
- 1/4 cup (60 ml) fresh basil, chopped (optional)

For Serving:

- Cooked spaghetti or other pasta
- Grated Parmesan cheese

Instructions:

1.Prepare the Meatballs:

-Preheat your oven to 400°F (200°C). Line a baking sheet with parchment paper.

-In a large bowl, combine the ground beef, ground pork, breadcrumbs, grated Parmesan cheese, minced garlic, milk, egg, chopped parsley, dried oregano, salt, black pepper, and red pepper flakes (if using).

-Mix gently until all ingredients are well combined. Avoid overmixing to keep the meatballs tender.

-Form the mixture into 1 1/2-inch (3.8 cm) meatballs and place them on the prepared baking sheet.

2.Bake the Meatballs:

-Bake the meatballs in the preheated oven for 15-20 minutes, or until they are browned and cooked through.

3.Prepare the Marinara Sauce:

-While the meatballs are baking, heat the olive oil in a large skillet over medium heat.

-Add the finely chopped onion and sauté until it becomes translucent

-Add the minced garlic and cook for another minute until fragrant.

-Stir in the crushed tomatoes, dried oregano, dried basil, salt, black pepper, and red pepper flakes (if using).

-Bring the sauce to a simmer and let it cook for 15-20 minutes

-If desired, stir in the chopped fresh basil just before serving.

4.Combine Meatballs and Sauce:

-Once the meatballs are cooked, add them to the marinara sauce and simmer for an additional 5-10 minutes to allow the flavors to meld.

5.Serve.

Messy Controller Nachos

These loaded nachos feature a bed of crispy tortilla chips smothered in melted cheese, seasoned ground beef, black beans, and jalapeños. Topped with fresh tomatoes, avocado, sour cream, and a sprinkle of cilantro, each bite offers a delicious explosion of flavors and textures. Perfect for game nights or casual gatherings, these nachos are the ideal messy and mouth-watering treat to keep you fueled and ready for victory.

Ingredients:

- 1 pound (450 g) ground beef
- 1 tablespoon (15 ml) olive oil
- 1 small onion, finely chopped
- 2 cloves garlic, minced
- 1 packet (1 ounce / 28 g) taco seasoning
- 1/2 cup (120 ml) water
- 1 can (15 ounces / 425 g) black beans, drained and rinsed (optional)
- 2 tablespoons (30 g) unsalted butter
- 2 tablespoons (15 g) all-purpose flour
- 1 cup (240 ml) milk
- 2 cups (200 g) shredded cheddar
- 1/2 teaspoon (2.5 g) salt
- 1/4 teaspoon (1.25 g) cayenne pepper (optional, for extra heat)

For Assembling the Nachos:

- 1 large bag of tortilla chips
- 1 cup (150 g) shredded lettuce
- 1 cup (150 g) diced tomatoes
- 1/2 cup (75 g) sliced jalapeños
- 1/2 cup (75 g) sliced black olives
- 1/2 cup (75 g) sour cream
- 1/4 cup (60 ml) fresh cilantro, chopped

Instructions:

-In a large skillet, heat the olive oil over medium-high heat.
-Add the finely chopped onion and sauté until translucent.
-Add the minced garlic and cook for another minute until fragrant.
-Add the ground beef to the skillet and cook until browned, breaking it up with a spoon as it cooks.
-Drain any excess fat.
-Stir in the taco seasoning mix and water. Add the black beans if using.
-Simmer for 5-7 minutes, until the sauce has thickened and the beef is well-coated with the seasoning.
-In a medium saucepan, melt the butter over medium heat.
-Stir in the flour and cook for 1-2 minutes to form a roux.
-Gradually whisk in the milk, continuing to stir until the mixture is smooth and starts to thicken.
-Add the shredded cheddar cheese, salt, and cayenne pepper (if using).
-Stir until the cheese is completely melted and the sauce is smooth.
-Preheat your oven to 350°F (175°C).
-Spread a layer of tortilla chips on a large baking sheet.
-Spoon the beef mixture evenly over the chips.
-Pour the cheese sauce over the beef and chips.
-Bake in the preheated oven for 10-15 minutes, until the nachos are heated through and the cheese is bubbly.
-Remove the nachos from the oven and top with shredded lettuce, diced tomatoes, sliced jalapeños, sliced black olives, and sour cream.
-Garnish with chopped fresh cilantro.
-Serve with salsa on the side if desired.

Pleasant Park Oven Pizza

Bring the cozy neighborhood vibes of Pleasant Park to your table with Pleasant Park Oven Pizza, inspired by the beloved Fortnite location. This homemade pizza features a crispy, golden crust topped with rich tomato sauce, gooey mozzarella cheese, and your favorite toppings. Whether you prefer classic pepperoni, fresh vegetables, or a gourmet combination, each slice is a delightful mix of savory flavors and textures.

Ingredients:

For the Pizza Dough:

- 3 1/2 to 4 cups (420-480 g) all-purpose flour
- 1 teaspoon (5 g) sugar
- 1 packet (2 1/4 teaspoons / 7 g) active dry yeast
- 2 teaspoons (10 g) salt
- 1 1/2 cups (360 ml) warm water (110°F / 45°C)
- 2 tablespoons (30 ml) olive oil

For the Pizza Sauce:

- 1 can (15 ounces / 425 g) tomato sauce
- 2 tablespoons (30 ml) olive oil
- 2 cloves garlic, minced
- 1 teaspoon (5 g) dried oregano
- 1 teaspoon (5 g) dried basil
- 1/2 teaspoon (2.5 g) salt
- 1/2 teaspoon (2.5 g) black pepper
- 1/4 teaspoon (1.25 g) red pepper flakes

For the Toppings:

- 2 cups (200 g) shredded mozzarella
- 1/2 cup (50 g) grated Parmesan cheese
- Various toppings: pepperoni, sliced mushrooms, bell peppers, onions, olives, fresh basil, etc.

Instructions:

-In a large bowl, combine the warm water, sugar, and yeast. Let it sit for 5-10 minutes until it becomes frothy.

-Add the olive oil, salt, and 3 1/2 cups of flour to the yeast mixture. Mix until a dough forms.

-Turn the dough out onto a floured surface and knead for about 8-10 minutes, adding more flour as necessary, until the dough is smooth.

-Place the dough in a lightly oiled bowl, cover it with a damp cloth, and let it rise in a warm place for about 1-2 hours, or until it has doubled.

-In a medium saucepan, heat the olive oil over medium heat.

-Add the minced garlic and sauté for about 1 minute until fragrant.

-Stir in the tomato sauce, dried oregano, dried basil, salt, black pepper, and red pepper flakes (if using).

-Bring the sauce to a simmer and let it cook for 15-20 minutes, stirring occasionally. Remove from heat and set aside.

-Punch down the risen dough and divide it into two equal portions.

-On a floured surface, roll out each portion of dough into a circle.

-Transfer the rolled-out dough to a pizza peel or baking sheet.

-Spread a thin layer of the prepared pizza sauce over the dough, leaving a small border around the edges.

-Sprinkle the shredded mozzarella cheese evenly over the sauce, followed by the grated Parmesan cheese.

-Add your desired toppings.

-Carefully transfer the assembled pizza to the preheated pizza stone or place the baking sheet in the oven at 475°F (245°C).

-Bake for 10-15 minutes, or until the crust is golden brown and the cheese is bubbly and melted and serve.

Shifty Shafts Shepherd's Pie

This classic dish features a savory filling of seasoned ground beef and vegetables, all simmered in a rich gravy, and topped with a layer of creamy mashed potatoes. Baked to golden perfection, each bite delivers a warm and satisfying blend of flavors and textures. Perfect for a cozy dinner, this shepherd's pie brings a touch of rustic charm and comfort to your table.

Ingredients:

For the Filling:

- 1 tablespoon (15 ml) olive oil
- 1 large onion, diced
- 2 cloves garlic, minced
- 1 pound (450 g) ground lamb or beef
- 2 large carrots, diced
- 1 cup (150 g) frozen peas
- 1 cup (150 g) frozen corn
- 2 tablespoons (30 ml) tomato paste
- 1 tablespoon (15 ml) Worcestershire sauce
- 1 cup (240 ml) beef or chicken broth
- 1 teaspoon (5 g) dried thyme
- 1 teaspoon (5 g) dried rosemary
- Salt and pepper to taste

For the Mashed Potato Topping:

- 2 pounds (900 g) potatoes, peeled and diced
- 1/2 cup (120 ml) milk
- 1/4 cup (60 g) unsalted butter
- 1/2 cup (60 g) grated Parmesan cheese (optional)
- Salt and pepper to taste

Instructions:

-Preheat your oven to 400°F (200°C).

-In a large skillet or sauté pan, heat the olive oil over medium-high heat.

-Add the diced onion and cook until it becomes translucent.

-Add the minced garlic and cook for another minute until fragrant.

-Add the ground lamb or beef to the pan and cook until browned, breaking it up with a spoon as it cooks. Drain any excess fat if necessary.

-Stir in the diced carrots and cook for 5 minutes.

-Add the tomato paste and Worcestershire sauce, stirring well to combine.

-Pour in the beef or chicken broth and add the dried thyme and rosemary. Stir to combine.

-Let the mixture simmer for 10 minutes until the sauce thickens slightly. Stir in the frozen peas and corn, and cook for another 2-3 minutes. Season with salt and pepper to taste.

-While the filling is simmering, place the diced potatoes in a large pot and cover with water. Add a pinch of salt and bring to a boil.

-Cook the potatoes until they are tender, about 15-20 minutes. Drain.---- Return the potatoes to the pot and mash with a potato masher or fork.

-Stir in the milk, butter, and grated Parmesan cheese and season.

-Transfer the filling to a large baking dish and spread.

-Spoon the mashed potatoes over the top of the filling, spreading them out to cover the entire surface. Use a fork to create a decorative pattern.

-Place the baking dish in the preheated oven and bake for 20-25 minutes, or until the top is golden brown and the filling is bubbling around the edges.

-Let the shepherd's pie cool for a few minutes before serving and serve.

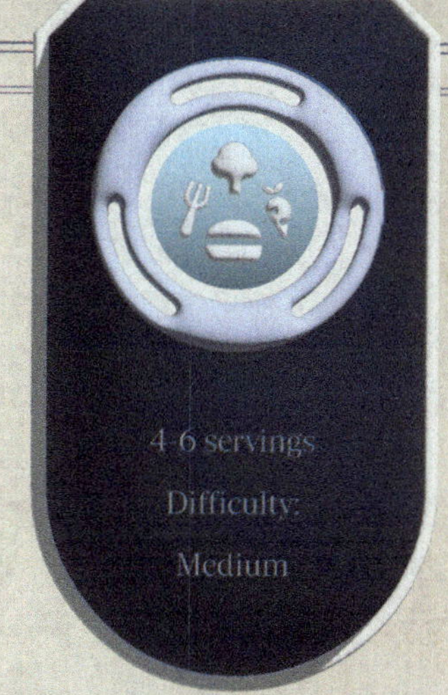

Sunny Steps Stir-fry

Brighten up your meal with Sunny Steps Stir-fry, inspired by the vibrant and lively atmosphere of Fortnite's Sunny Steps. This colorful dish features an array of fresh vegetables and tender pieces of chicken or tofu, all quickly stir-fried in a hot pan and tossed with a savory soy-ginger sauce. Bursting with flavor and nutrients, this stir-fry is perfect for a quick and healthy dinner that will keep you energized and ready for your next adventure. Serve it over steamed rice or noodles for a complete and satisfying meal.

Ingredients:

For the Stir-fry:

- 1 block (14 ounces / 400 g) firm tofu
- 2 tablespoons (30 ml) soy sauce
- 1 tablespoon (15 ml) sesame oil
- 2 tablespoons (30 ml) vegetable oil
- 1 red bell pepper, sliced
- 1 yellow bell pepper, sliced
- 1 cup (150 g) broccoli florets
- 1 carrot, julienned
- 1 zucchini, sliced
- 1 cup (150 g) snap peas
- 3 cloves garlic, minced
- 1 tablespoon (15 g) fresh ginger

For the Sauce:

- 1/4 cup (60 ml) soy sauce
- 2 tablespoons (30 ml) hoisin sauce
- 1 tablespoon (15 ml) rice vinegar
- 1 tablespoon (15 ml) honey or maple syrup
- 1 teaspoon (5 ml) sesame oil
- 1 tablespoon (8 g) cornstarch

For Serving:

- Cooked rice or noodles
- Sesame seeds
- Sliced green onions
- Lime wedges

Instructions:

1.Prepare the Tofu:

-Press the tofu to remove excess moisture by wrapping it in paper towels and placing a heavy object on top for about 15 minutes.

-Cut the tofu into cubes and marinate with 2 tablespoons soy sauce and 1 tablespoon sesame oil for 10 minutes.

2.Cook the Tofu:

-Heat 1 tablespoon vegetable oil in a large skillet or wok over medium-high heat.

-Add the marinated tofu and cook until golden brown on all sides, about 5-7 minutes. Remove from the skillet and set aside.

3.Prepare the Vegetables:

-In the same skillet, add the remaining 1 tablespoon vegetable oil.

-Add the minced garlic and fresh ginger, and sauté for 1-2 minutes until fragrant.

-Add the sliced bell peppers, broccoli, carrot, zucchini, and snap peas. Stir-fry for 5-7 minutes until the vegetables are tender-crisp.

4.Prepare the Sauce:

-In a small bowl, whisk together the soy sauce, hoisin sauce, rice vinegar, honey or maple syrup, sesame oil, water, and cornstarch until smooth.

5.Combine and Cook:

-Return the cooked tofu to the skillet with the vegetables.

-Pour the sauce over the tofu and vegetables. Stir well to coat everything evenly.

-Cook for an additional 2-3 minutes until the sauce has thickened and everything is heated through.

6.Serve.

Supply Drop Sandwich

Unlock the ultimate meal with the Supply Drop Sandwich, inspired by the exciting and rewarding supply drops. This sandwich is packed with layers of flavorful deli meats, crisp lettuce, juicy tomatoes, tangy pickles, and creamy cheese, all nestled between slices of freshly baked bread. Each bite delivers a satisfying mix of textures and tastes, making it the perfect choice for a quick lunch or a satisfying snack.

Ingredients:

For the Sandwich:

- 8 slices of whole grain or sourdough bread
- 8 ounces (225 g) deli-sliced turkey breast
- 8 slices of cooked bacon
- 1 avocado, sliced
- 1 large tomato, sliced
- 4 leaves of lettuce (romaine or iceberg)
- 4 slices of cheddar cheese
- 2 tablespoons (30 ml) mayonnaise
- 1 tablespoon (15 ml) Dijon mustard
- Salt and pepper to taste

Instructions:

1.Prepare the Ingredients:

-Cook the bacon until crispy and drain on paper towels.

-Slice the avocado, tomato, and cheese.

-Wash and dry the lettuce leaves.

2.Toast the Bread:

-Lightly toast the bread slices until they are golden brown.

3.Assemble the Sandwich:

-Lay out 4 slices of toasted bread. Spread a thin layer of mayonnaise on each slice.

-On each of these slices, layer lettuce, turkey breast, and a slice of cheddar cheese.

-Top each with another slice of toasted bread. Spread a thin layer of Dijon mustard on these slices.

-Add slices of avocado, bacon, and tomato on top of the mustard layer. Sprinkle with a little salt and pepper.

-Place the final slice of toasted bread on top of each sandwich.

4.Secure the Sandwich:

-For a traditional club sandwich look, use toothpicks to secure the sandwich layers. You can cut each sandwich into halves or quarters, depending on your preference.

5.Serve:

-Arrange the sandwiches on a serving platter. For a true Fortnite Supply Drop theme, you can wrap each sandwich with a blue napkin or place them in blue sandwich wrappers.

"That-Friend-Who-Plays-REAL-Bad" Moussaka

Celebrate the fun and camaraderie of gaming nights with a dish inspired by the good times and laughs shared with friends who might not be the best at gaming, but always bring the best vibes. This Greek classic features layers of tender eggplant, seasoned ground beef, and rich béchamel sauce, all baked to golden perfection. Each slice offers a comforting and delicious blend of flavors, perfect for sharing and enjoying together, no matter how the game goes.

6-8 servings
Difficulty:
Difficult

Ingredients:

For the Eggplant Layers:

- 2 large eggplants, sliced into 1/4-inch (0.6 cm) rounds
- Olive oil for brushing

For the Meat Sauce:

- 1 pound (450 g) ground lamb or beef
- 1 large onion, finely chopped
- 3 cloves garlic, minced
- 1 can (14.5 ounces / 410 g) diced tomatoes
- 2 tablespoons (30 g) tomato paste
- 1/2 cup (120 ml) red wine (optional)
- 1 teaspoon (5 g) ground cinnamon
- 1 teaspoon (5 g) ground allspice
- 1 teaspoon (5 g) dried oregano
- 1 teaspoon (5 g) dried thyme

For the Béchamel Sauce:

- 4 tablespoons (60 g) unsalted butter
- 1/4 cup (30 g) all-purpose flour
- 2 cups (480 ml) whole milk
- 1/4 teaspoon (1.25 g) ground nutmeg
- Salt and pepper to taste
- 1/2 cup (50 g) grated Parmesan cheese
- 2 large eggs, beaten

Instructions:

-Sprinkle the eggplant slices with salt and let them sit in a colander for about 30 minutes to draw out excess moisture.

-Rinse the slices under cold water and pat them dry with paper towels.

-Brush both sides of the eggplant slices with olive oil and place them on the prepared baking sheet.

-Roast the eggplant slices for about 20 minutes, flipping halfway through, until they are tender and lightly browned.

-In a large skillet, cook the ground lamb or beef over medium-high heat.

-Add the finely chopped onion and minced garlic to the skillet and sauté.

-Stir in the diced tomatoes, tomato paste, red wine (if using), ground cinnamon, ground allspice, dried oregano, dried thyme, salt, and pepper.

-Reduce the heat to low and let the sauce simmer for about 20 minutes, stirring occasionally. Remove from heat and set aside.

-In a medium saucepan, melt the butter over medium heat.

-Whisk in the flour and cook for 1-2 minutes to form a roux.

-Gradually whisk in the milk, continuing to stir until it is smooth.

-Season the béchamel sauce with ground nutmeg, salt, and pepper. Stir in the grated Parmesan cheese until melted.

-Once cooled, whisk in the beaten eggs until well combined.

-Arrange a layer of roasted eggplant slices at the bottom of baking dish.

-Spread half of the meat sauce over the eggplant layer.

-Add another layer of eggplant slices on top of the meat sauce.

-Spread the remaining meat sauce over the second layer of eggplant.

-Pour the béchamel sauce over the top, spreading it evenly with a spatula. Bake in the preheated oven for about 45-50 minutes, or until the top is golden brown and the sauce is bubbling and serve!

Tilted Towers Tenders

4 servings
Difficulty:
Medium

Step up your snack game with Tilted Towers Tenders, inspired by the high-stakes excitement of Fortnite's Tilted Towers. These crispy chicken tenders are seasoned to perfection and fried until golden brown, offering a satisfying crunch with every bite. Perfect for dipping in your favorite sauces, these tenders are an ideal treat for game nights, parties, or anytime you crave a delicious and hearty snack. Easy to make and impossible to resist, Tilted Towers Tenders will keep you energized and ready for the next battle.

Ingredients:

For the Chicken Tenders:

- 1 pound (450 g) chicken tenders or boneless, skinless chicken breasts cut into strips
- 1 cup (240 ml) buttermilk
- 1 teaspoon (5 g) salt
- 1/2 teaspoon (2.5 g) black pepper
- 1/2 teaspoon (2.5 g) garlic powder
- 1/2 teaspoon (2.5 g) onion powder
- 1/2 teaspoon (2.5 g) paprika
- 1/4 teaspoon (1.25 g) cayenne pepper (optional, for extra heat)

For the Breading:

- 1 1/2 cups (180 g) all-purpose flour
- 1/2 cup (60 g) cornstarch
- 1 teaspoon (5 g) salt
- 1/2 teaspoon (2.5 g) black pepper
- 1/2 teaspoon (2.5 g) garlic powder
- 1/2 teaspoon (2.5 g) onion powder
- 1/2 teaspoon (2.5 g) paprika

For Frying:

- Vegetable oil, for frying

For Serving:

- Ranch or honey mustard dipping sauce
- Lemon wedges (optional)

Instructions:

-In a large bowl, combine the chicken tenders, buttermilk, salt, black pepper, garlic powder, onion powder, paprika, and cayenne pepper.

-Mix well to ensure the chicken is evenly coated.

-Cover and refrigerate for at least 30 minutes, or up to 4 hours for best results.

-In a shallow dish, whisk together the flour, cornstarch, salt, black pepper, garlic powder, onion powder, and paprika.

3.Bread the Chicken:

-Remove the chicken tenders from the buttermilk marinade, allowing any excess to drip off.

-Dredge each chicken tender in the flour mixture, pressing lightly to adhere. Shake off any excess flour.

-Place the breaded chicken tenders on a baking sheet or plate and let them rest for 10-15 minutes. This helps the breading adhere better during frying.

-In a large, deep skillet or Dutch oven, heat about 2 inches (5 cm) of vegetable oil to 350°F (175°C). Use a thermometer to maintain the temperature.

-Working in batches, carefully place the breaded chicken tenders into the hot oil. Fry for 4-5 minutes per side, or until the chicken is golden brown and cooked through, with an internal temperature of 165°F (74°C).

-Use a slotted spoon or tongs to transfer the fried chicken tenders to a paper towel-lined plate to drain excess oil.

-Arrange the Tilted Towers Tenders on a serving platter.

-Serve with ranch or honey mustard dipping sauce and lemon wedges, if desired.

Tomato Town Torte

Indulge in the sweet and savory flavors of Tomato Town Torte, inspired by the iconic Tomato Town of Fortnite. This unique dessert features layers of flaky pastry filled with a rich tomato jam, creamy mascarpone, and fresh basil, creating a delightful harmony of flavors. Each bite offers a perfect balance of sweetness and a hint of savory, making it an intriguing and delicious treat for any occasion. Perfect for impressing guests or enjoying as a special dessert, Tomato Town Torte brings a gourmet touch to your culinary adventures.

Ingredients:

For the Crust:

- 1 1/4 cups (150 g) all-purpose flour
- 1/2 teaspoon (2.5 g) salt
- 1/2 cup (115 g) unsalted butter, cold and cubed
- 1/4 cup (60 ml) ice water

For the Filling:

- 4-5 medium tomatoes, sliced
- 1 teaspoon (5 g) salt (for draining tomatoes)
- 1 cup (240 ml) ricotta cheese
- 1/2 cup (120 ml) shredded mozzarella cheese
- 1/4 cup (25 g) grated Parmesan cheese
- 1/4 cup (60 ml) fresh basil leaves, chopped
- 2 cloves garlic, minced
- 1 tablespoon (15 ml) olive oil
- Salt and pepper to taste
- Fresh basil leaves for garnish
- Balsamic glaze for drizzling (optional)

Instructions:

-In a large bowl, combine the flour and salt. Add the cold, cubed butter and use a pastry cutter or your fingers to mix until the mixture resembles coarse crumbs.

-Gradually add the ice water, one tablespoon at a time, mixing until the dough comes together.

-Form the dough into a disk, wrap it in plastic wrap, and refrigerate for at least 30 minutes.

-While the dough is chilling, place the tomato slices on a paper towel-lined baking sheet. Sprinkle with 1 teaspoon of salt and let them sit for 20-30 minutes to draw out excess moisture.

-After 30 minutes, pat the tomatoes dry with paper towels.

-Preheat your oven to 375°F (190°C).

-In a medium bowl, combine the ricotta cheese, shredded mozzarella cheese, grated Parmesan cheese, chopped basil leaves, and minced garlic. Mix well.

-On a lightly floured surface, roll out the chilled dough into a circle about 12 inches (30 cm) in diameter.

-Transfer the dough to a tart pan or a baking sheet lined with parchment paper.

-Spread the cheese mixture evenly over the dough, leaving a 1-inch (2.5 cm) border around the edges.

-Arrange the tomato slices on top of the cheese mixture.

-Fold the edges of the dough over the filling, pleating as necessary.

-Brush the edges of the dough with olive oil and season the tomatoes.

-Bake in the preheated oven for 35-40 minutes, or until the crust is golden brown and the filling is bubbly and serve.

Tycoon Tacos

These tacos are loaded with premium ingredients, featuring juicy, marinated steak or chicken, fresh avocado slices, tangy pickled red onions, and a sprinkle of queso fresco. Wrapped in soft, warm tortillas and drizzled with a zesty lime crema, each bite is a luxurious explosion of flavors. Perfect for a fancy dinner or a gourmet twist on taco night, Tycoon Tacos will elevate your dining experience to legendary status.

4-6 servings
Difficulty:
Easy

Ingredients:

- 1 pound (450 g) ground beef or ground turkey
- 1 tablespoon (15 ml) olive oil
- 1 small onion, finely chopped
- 2 cloves garlic, minced
- 1 packet (1 ounce / 28 g) taco seasoning mix (or homemade mix: 1 tablespoon chili powder, 1 teaspoon ground cumin, 1 teaspoon smoked paprika, 1/2 teaspoon garlic powder, 1/2 teaspoon onion powder, 1/4 teaspoon dried oregano, 1/4 teaspoon crushed red pepper flakes, 1/4 teaspoon salt)
- 1/2 cup (120 ml) water
- 8-10 small corn or flour tortillas
- 1 cup (150 g) shredded lettuce
- 1 cup (150 g) diced tomatoes
- 1/2 cup (75 g) diced red onion
- 1 cup (150 g) shredded cheddar or
- 1/2 cup (120 ml) sour cream
- 1/2 cup (120 ml) guacamole
- Fresh cilantro leaves for garnish
- Lime wedges for serving
- Sliced jalapeños
- Sliced black olives
- Salsa

Instructions:

1.Prepare the Taco Meat:

-In a large skillet, heat the olive oil over medium-high heat.

-Add the finely chopped onion and sauté until translucent, about 5 minutes.

-Add the minced garlic and cook for another minute until fragrant.

-Add the ground beef or turkey to the skillet, breaking it up with a spoon as it cooks. Cook until browned and fully cooked, about 7-8 minutes. Drain any excess fat if necessary.

-Stir in the taco seasoning mix and water. Bring to a simmer and cook for 3-4 minutes, until the sauce thickens and the meat is well-coated with the seasoning.

2.Warm the Tortillas:

-While the taco meat is simmering, warm the tortillas in a dry skillet over medium heat, or wrap them in a damp paper towel and microwave for about 30 seconds to make them pliable.

3.Assemble the Tacos:

-Place a generous spoonful of the taco meat onto each warm tortilla.

-Top with shredded lettuce, diced tomatoes, diced red onion, and shredded cheese.

-Add a dollop of sour cream and guacamole to each taco.

-.Garnish and Serve:

-Garnish with fresh cilantro leaves and serve with lime wedges on the side.

-Offer optional toppings like sliced jalapeños, sliced black olives, salsa, and hot sauce for guests to customize their tacos.

Desserts

Boogie Bomb Brownies

12 servings
Difficulty:
Easy

Get ready to dance with delight with Boogie Bomb Brownies, inspired by the fun and chaos of Fortnite's Boogie Bombs. These rich, fudgy brownies are packed with chocolatey goodness and a surprise twist – colorful sprinkles or chocolate chips that explode with flavor in every bite. Perfect for parties, gaming sessions, or just a sweet treat, these brownies will have everyone grooving with joy. Easy to make and impossible to resist, Boogie Bomb Brownies are a guaranteed hit for any occasion.

For the Brownies:

•1/2 cup (115 g) unsalted butter
•1 cup (200 g) granulated sugar
•2 large eggs
•1 teaspoon (5 ml) vanilla extract
•1/3 cup (40 g) unsweetened cocoa powder
•1/2 cup (65 g) all-purpose flour
•1/4 teaspoon (1.25 g) salt
•1/4 teaspoon (1.25 g) baking powder
•1/2 cup (90 g) chocolate chips or chunks

For the Topping:

•1/4 cup (60 ml) heavy cream
•1/2 cup (90 g) semi-sweet chocolate chips or chunks
•Colorful sprinkles

Instructions:

-Preheat your oven to 350°F (175°C). Grease an 8x8-inch (20x20 cm) baking pan or line it with parchment paper.

-In a medium saucepan, melt the butter over low heat. Remove from heat and stir in the sugar, eggs, and vanilla extract until well combined.

-In a separate bowl, whisk together the cocoa powder, flour, salt, and baking powder.

-Gradually add the dry ingredients to the butter mixture, stirring until just combined. Do not overmix.

-Fold in the chocolate chips or chunks.

-Pour the batter into the prepared baking pan, spreading it evenly.

-Bake in the preheated oven for 20-25 minutes, or until a toothpick inserted into the center comes out with a few moist crumbs. Do not overbake; the brownies should be fudgy.

-Allow the brownies to cool completely in the pan on a wire rack.

-In a small saucepan, heat the heavy cream over medium heat until it just begins to simmer. Remove from heat.

-Add the chocolate chips or chunks to the hot cream, stirring until the chocolate is completely melted and smooth.

-Pour the chocolate ganache over the cooled brownies, spreading it evenly with a spatula.

-Allow the ganache to set at room temperature or refrigerate the brownies for a quicker set.

-Once the ganache is set, cut the brownies into squares.

Campfire S'mores

Warm up with the nostalgic taste of Campfire S'mores! These classic treats feature gooey, melted marshmallows and rich chocolate sandwiched between crunchy graham crackers, perfectly capturing the essence of a night under the stars. Whether you're enjoying them by a real campfire or in the comfort of your kitchen, these s'mores bring a touch of outdoor adventure to your snacking experience. Ideal for sharing with friends or as a sweet ending to a meal, Campfire S'mores are a delightful and timeless treat.

Ingredients:

•8 graham crackers, broken in half (to make 16 squares)

•8 large marshmallows

•2 milk chocolate bars (about 3 ounces each), broken into pieces that fit the graham crackers

Instructions:

1.Prepare the Ingredients:

-Break the graham crackers in half to make 16 squares.

-Break the chocolate bars into pieces that will fit on the graham crackers.

2.Roast the Marshmallows:

-Using a long skewer or roasting stick, roast the marshmallows over an open flame (campfire, grill, or even a gas stove burner) until golden brown and gooey. Turn the marshmallows slowly to ensure even roasting.

3.Assemble the S'mores:

-Place a piece of chocolate on top of a graham cracker square.

-Carefully place the hot roasted marshmallow on top of the chocolate.

-Top with another graham cracker square and gently press down to melt the chocolate and sandwich the marshmallow.

4.Serve Immediately:

-Enjoy your s'mores while they're warm and gooey!

Campfire S'mores

Power up your snack game with Carbide's Caramel Apples, inspired by the sleek and strong character of Fortnite's Carbide. These delicious treats feature crisp, juicy apples coated in a rich, buttery caramel, offering a perfect balance of sweetness and tartness. Ideal for parties, game nights, or a fun dessert, these caramel apples bring a touch of epic flair to any occasion. Easy to make and even easier to enjoy, Carbide's Caramel Apples are a heroic treat that will energize your taste buds.

Ingredients:

•6 medium apples (Granny Smith, Honeycrisp, or your favorite variety)
•6 wooden sticks or popsicle sticks
•1 cup (200 g) granulated sugar
•1/2 cup (120 ml) light corn syrup
•1/2 cup (120 ml) heavy cream
•1/4 cup (60 ml) unsalted butter
•1 teaspoon (5 ml) vanilla extract
•1/4 teaspoon (1.25 g) salt
•Optional toppings: chopped nuts, sprinkles, mini chocolate chips, crushed cookies

Instructions:

1.Prepare the Apples:

-Wash and thoroughly dry the apples. Remove the stems and insert a wooden stick into the top of each apple.

-Line a baking sheet with parchment paper and lightly grease it with butter or cooking spray to prevent sticking.

2.Make the Caramel:

-In a medium saucepan, combine the granulated sugar, light corn syrup, heavy cream, unsalted butter, and salt.

-Cook over medium heat, stirring constantly, until the mixture reaches 245°F (118°C) on a candy thermometer. This will take about 10-15 minutes. Be careful not to let it burn.

-Remove the saucepan from heat and stir in the vanilla extract.

3.Dip the Apples:

-Working quickly, dip each apple into the hot caramel, tilting the pan as needed to fully coat the apple. Allow any excess caramel to drip off back into the pan.

-Immediately roll the caramel-coated apple in your desired toppings, if using.

-Place the coated apples on the prepared baking sheet to set.

4.Let the Caramel Set:

-Allow the caramel apples to cool and set completely at room temperature. This will take about 30 minutes to 1 hour.

5.Serve:

-Once the caramel has set, your caramel apples are ready to enjoy! They can be stored in the refrigerator for up to 3 days.

Crackshot Cookies

These delightful gingerbread cookies are spiced just right with ginger, cinnamon, and nutmeg, then baked to a perfect crispness. Decorate them with royal icing to bring your favorite Fortnite characters to life, making them as fun to create as they are to eat. Perfect for holiday gatherings, gaming sessions, or simply indulging your sweet tooth, Crackshot Cookies are sure to add a whimsical and delicious touch to your celebrations.

6-10 servings
Difficulty:
Medium

Ingredients:

For the Cookies:

- 3 cups (360 g) all-purpose flour
- 3/4 cup (150 g) brown sugar, packed
- 3/4 cup (180 ml) unsalted butter, softened
- 1/2 cup (120 ml) molasses
- 1 large egg
- 1 teaspoon (5 ml) vanilla extract
- 1 teaspoon (5 g) baking soda
- 1/2 teaspoon (2.5 g) salt
- 1 tablespoon (15 g) ground ginger
- 1 tablespoon (15 g) ground cinnamon
- 1/2 teaspoon (2.5 g) ground cloves
- 1/2 teaspoon (2.5 g) ground nutmeg

For the Icing:

- 2 cups (240 g) powdered sugar
- 1-2 tablespoons (15-30 ml) milk or water
- 1 tablespoon (15 ml) light corn syrup (optional, for shine)
- 1/2 teaspoon (2.5 ml) vanilla extract
- Food coloring (optional)

Instructions:

-In a large bowl, sift together the flour, baking soda, salt, ground ginger, ground cinnamon, ground cloves, and ground nutmeg. Set aside.

-In a separate large bowl, beat the softened butter and brown sugar together until light and fluffy.

-Add the molasses, egg, and vanilla extract to the butter mixture, and beat until well combined.

-Gradually add the dry ingredients to the wet ingredients, mixing until the dough comes together.

-Divide the dough into two equal portions, flatten them into disks, and wrap them in plastic wrap.

-Refrigerate for at least 2 hours or overnight to firm up the dough.

-Preheat your oven to 350°F (175°C).

-Line two baking sheets with parchment paper.

-On a lightly floured surface, roll out one disk of dough to about 1/4-inch (0.6 cm) thickness.

-Use cookie cutters to cut out gingerbread men or other festive shapes.

-Transfer the cookies to the prepared baking sheets, spacing them apart.

-Bake in the preheated oven for 8-10 minutes, or until the edges are set and the cookies are lightly browned.

-Remove from the oven and let the cookies cool on the baking sheets for 5 minutes before transferring them to a wire rack to cool completely.

-In a medium bowl, whisk together the powdered sugar, 1 tablespoon of milk or water, light corn syrup (if using), and vanilla extract. Add more milk or water as needed to reach your desired consistency.

-If using food coloring, divide the icing into separate bowls and add food coloring as desired. Let it cool and serve.

Crit Truffles

These luxurious chocolate truffles are made from rich, creamy ganache, coated in a variety of toppings like cocoa powder, crushed nuts, or shredded coconut. Each bite delivers an intense burst of chocolate flavor, making them the perfect treat for a special occasion or a well-deserved reward after a tough game. Easy to make and elegantly delicious, Crit Truffles will elevate your dessert game to legendary status.

Ingredients:

- 8 ounces (225 g) high-quality dark chocolate (70% cocoa), finely chopped
- 1/2 cup (120 ml) heavy cream
- 2 tablespoons (30 g) unsalted butter, cut into small pieces
- 1 teaspoon (5 ml) vanilla extract
- Cocoa powder, for coating
- Optional: finely chopped nuts, shredded coconut, or sprinkles for coating

Instructions:

1.Prepare the Chocolate:

-Place the finely chopped dark chocolate in a heatproof bowl.

2.Heat the Cream:

-In a small saucepan, heat the heavy cream over medium heat until it just begins to simmer. Do not let it boil.

3.Combine Cream and Chocolate:

-Pour the hot cream over the chopped chocolate. Let it sit for 2-3 minutes to allow the chocolate to melt.

-Gently stir the mixture until smooth and glossy.

4.Add Butter and Vanilla:

-Add the small pieces of butter and the vanilla extract to the chocolate mixture.

-Stir until the butter is completely melted and incorporated.

5.Chill the Mixture:

-Cover the bowl with plastic wrap and refrigerate for at least 2 hours, or until the mixture is firm enough to scoop.

6.Shape the Truffles:

-Using a small cookie scoop or a teaspoon, scoop out small portions of the chocolate mixture and roll them into balls between your palms.

7.Coat the Truffles:

-Roll each truffle in cocoa powder to coat evenly. Alternatively, you can roll them in finely chopped nuts, shredded coconut, or sprinkles for different flavors and textures.

8.Store and Serve:

-Place the coated truffles on a baking sheet lined with parchment paper.

-Refrigerate the truffles for another 30 minutes to set.

Dusty Divot Donuts

Indulge in the sweet and satisfying taste of Dusty Divot Donuts, inspired by the iconic Fortnite location. These classic donuts are light, fluffy, and perfectly fried to golden perfection, then dipped in a sweet glaze that's sure to please. With a soft interior and a crispy exterior, these donuts are a delicious treat for any time of day. Whether you're enjoying them with a morning coffee or as an afternoon snack, Dusty Divot Donuts are the perfect way to satisfy your sweet tooth and bring a touch of Fortnite fun to your kitchen.

Ingredients:

For the Donuts:

- 2 1/4 teaspoons (1 packet / 7 g) active dry yeast
- 1/4 cup (60 ml) warm water (about 110°F / 45°C)
- 3/4 cup (180 ml) warm milk (about 110°F / 45°C)
- 1/4 cup (50 g) granulated sugar
- 1/2 teaspoon (2.5 g) salt
- 1/4 cup (60 g) unsalted butter, softened
- 1 large egg
- 3 1/2 cups (420 g) all-purpose flour, plus more for rolling out
- Vegetable oil, for frying

For the Glaze:

- 2 cups (240 g) powdered sugar
- 1/4 cup (60 ml) milk
- 1 teaspoon (5 ml) vanilla extract

Instructions:

-In a small bowl, dissolve the active dry yeast in warm water. Let it sit for about 5 minutes until it becomes frothy.

-In a large mixing bowl, combine the warm milk, granulated sugar, salt, softened butter, and egg. Mix well.

-Add the frothy yeast mixture to the bowl and mix until combined.

-Gradually add the flour, 1 cup at a time, mixing until a soft dough forms. The dough should be slightly sticky but manageable.

-Turn the dough out onto a floured surface and knead for about 5-7 minutes until it becomes smooth and elastic.

-Place the dough in a greased bowl, cover it with a clean kitchen towel, and let it rise in a warm place for about 1-2 hours.

-Once the dough has risen, punch it down to release the air.

-Turn the dough out onto a floured surface and roll it out to 1/2-inch.

-Use a donut cutter or two round cookie cutters (one larger and one smaller) to cut out the donuts and donut holes. Re-roll the scraps.

-Place the cut-out donuts and donut holes on a baking sheet lined with parchment paper. Cover with a clean kitchen towel and let them rise for another 30 minutes, or until they have doubled in size.

-In a large, deep pot, heat vegetable oil to 350°F (175°C). The oil should be about 2-3 inches (5-7 cm) deep.

-Carefully place a few donuts at a time into the hot oil, frying for about 1-2 minutes per side, or until they are golden brown.

-Use a slotted spoon to transfer the fried donuts to a paper towel-lined plate to drain any excess oil.

-In a medium bowl, whisk together the powdered sugar, milk, and vanilla extract until smooth and dip the donuts. Enjoy!

Fudgy Fudge

This classic dessert features smooth, velvety fudge that melts in your mouth with each bite. Made from high-quality chocolate, sweetened condensed milk, and a touch of vanilla, it's the perfect balance of sweetness and indulgence. Ideal for gifting, sharing at gatherings, or enjoying as a personal reward, Fudgy Fudge is a timeless favorite that brings a touch of luxury to your dessert table.

Ingredients:

•3 cups (525 g) semisweet chocolate chips

•1 can (14 ounces / 395 g) sweetened condensed milk

•1/4 cup (60 g) unsalted butter, cut into pieces

•1 teaspoon (5 ml) vanilla extract

•1/4 teaspoon (1.25 g) salt

•Optional: 1/2 cup (60 g) chopped nuts, sprinkles, or other mix-ins

Instructions:

1.Prepare the Pan:

-Line an 8x8-inch (20x20 cm) baking pan with parchment paper, leaving some overhang on the sides to easily lift out the fudge later.

2.Melt the Ingredients:

-In a medium saucepan, combine the chocolate chips, sweetened condensed milk, and butter.

-Heat over medium-low heat, stirring constantly until the chocolate is completely melted and the mixture is smooth.

3.Add Flavoring:

-Remove the saucepan from the heat.

-Stir in the vanilla extract and salt until well combined.

-If using any mix-ins like chopped nuts or sprinkles, fold them in now.

4.Pour and Set:

-Pour the mixture into the prepared baking pan.

-Smooth the top with a spatula to ensure it is evenly distributed.

-Let the fudge cool to room temperature, then refrigerate for at least 2 hours or until firm.

5.Cut and Serve:

-Once the fudge is set, use the parchment paper overhang to lift it out of the pan.

-Cut into squares with a sharp knife.

6.Store:

-Store the fudge in an airtight container at room temperature for up to 2 weeks, or refrigerate for longer shelf life.

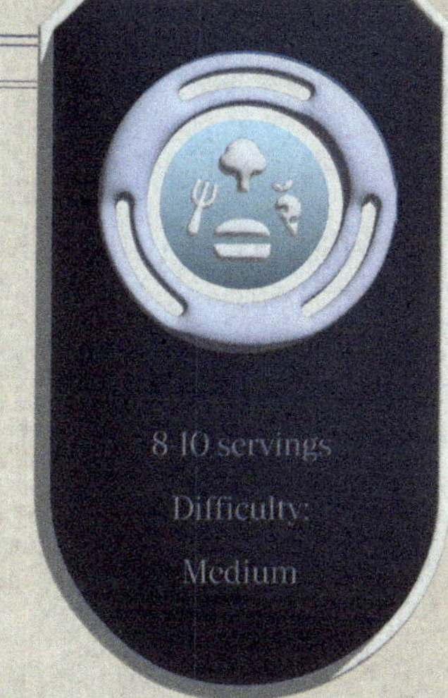

GG Cake

Flip your dessert game with the tropical delight of Pineapple Upside-Down Cake, inspired by the vibrant and playful world of Fortnite. This classic cake features a buttery, caramelized pineapple topping with maraschino cherries, perfectly complementing the moist and tender vanilla cake beneath. Each slice offers a delicious blend of fruity sweetness and rich flavor, making it an irresistible treat for any occasion. Ideal for parties, celebrations, or a sweet escape, Pineapple Upside-Down Cake brings a burst of sunshine to your dessert table.

Ingredients:

For the Topping:

- 1/4 cup (60 g) unsalted butter
- 1/2 cup (100 g) packed brown sugar
- 8-10 pineapple slices (canned or fresh)
- Maraschino cherries (optional)

For the Cake:

- 1 1/2 cups (190 g) all-purpose flour
- 1 cup (200 g) granulated sugar
- 1/2 cup (115 g) unsalted butter, softened
- 2 large eggs
- 1/2 cup (120 ml) pineapple juice (reserved from the canned pineapple or fresh)
- 1 teaspoon (5 ml) vanilla extract
- 1 1/2 teaspoons (7 g) baking powder
- 1/4 teaspoon (1.25 g) salt

Instructions:

-Preheat your oven to 350°F (175°C).

-In a 9-inch (23 cm) round cake pan, melt 1/4 cup of unsalted butter over low heat.

-Once the butter is melted, remove the pan from heat and evenly sprinkle 1/2 cup of packed brown sugar over the melted butter.

-Arrange the pineapple slices in a single layer over the brown sugar mixture. Place a maraschino cherry in the center of each pineapple slice if desired.

-In a medium bowl, whisk together the all-purpose flour, baking powder, and salt. Set aside.

-In a large mixing bowl, cream together 1/2 cup of softened unsalted butter and 1 cup of granulated sugar until light and fluffy.

-Add the eggs, one at a time, beating well after each addition.

-Stir in the vanilla extract.

-Gradually add the flour mixture to the butter mixture, alternating with the pineapple juice, beginning and ending with the flour mixture. Mix until just combined.

-Pour the cake batter over the pineapple slices in the cake pan.

-Bake in the preheated oven for 35-40 minutes, or until a toothpick inserted into the center of the cake comes out clean.

-Remove the cake from the oven and let it cool in the pan on a wire rack for about 10 minutes.

-Run a knife around the edges of the cake to loosen it from the pan.

-Place a serving plate over the cake pan and carefully invert the cake.

-Let the pan sit over the cake for a few minutes to allow the topping to drizzle over the cake. Let it cool and serve!

Love Ranger's Lava Cake

Ignite your passion for dessert with Love Ranger's Lava Cake, inspired by Fortnite's charming and steadfast Love Ranger. These individual chocolate cakes boast a warm, molten center that flows with rich, gooey chocolate when you cut into them. Each bite is a heavenly combination of soft cake and luscious molten filling, creating an indulgent and romantic treat. Perfect for special occasions, date nights, or just to satisfy your sweet tooth, Love Ranger's Lava Cake is a dessert that promises to melt hearts and delight taste buds.

Ingredients:

- 1/2 cup (115 g) unsalted butter, plus extra for greasing
- 4 ounces (115 g) high-quality dark chocolate, chopped
- 1 cup (120 g) powdered sugar
- 2 large eggs
- 2 large egg yolks
- 1 teaspoon (5 ml) vanilla extract
- 1/4 cup (30 g) all-purpose flour
- Pinch of salt
- Optional: cocoa powder or powdered sugar for dusting
- Optional: vanilla ice cream or whipped cream for serving

Instructions:

1.Prepare the Ramekins:

-Preheat your oven to 425°F (220°C).

-Grease four 6-ounce (180 ml) ramekins with butter and dust with cocoa powder or flour to prevent sticking. Tap out any excess cocoa powder or flour.

2.Melt the Chocolate and Butter:

-In a microwave-safe bowl, combine the chopped dark chocolate and 1/2 cup of unsalted butter. Microwave in 30-second intervals, stirring after each, until the chocolate and butter are completely melted and smooth. Alternatively, you can melt them together in a heatproof bowl set over a pot of simmering water.

3.Mix the Batter:

-In a medium mixing bowl, whisk together the powdered sugar, eggs, egg yolks, and vanilla extract until well combined.

-Gradually add the melted chocolate mixture to the egg mixture, stirring constantly to combine.

-Sift the all-purpose flour and a pinch of salt into the chocolate mixture, and gently fold until just combined.

4.Fill the Ramekins:

-Evenly divide the batter among the prepared ramekins.

5.Bake the Lava Cakes:

-Place the ramekins on a baking sheet and bake in the preheated oven for 12-14 minutes, or until the edges are set but the centers are still soft and jiggly.

-Remove from the oven and let the cakes cool in the ramekins for 1 minutes and serve.

Marshmellooo Meringue

Ignite your passion for dessert with Love Ranger's Lava Cake, inspired by Fortnite's charming and steadfast Love Ranger. These individual chocolate cakes boast a warm, molten center that flows with rich, gooey chocolate when you cut into them. Each bite is a heavenly combination of soft cake and luscious molten filling, creating an indulgent and romantic treat. Perfect for special occasions, date nights, or just to satisfy your sweet tooth, Love Ranger's Lava Cake is a dessert that promises to melt hearts and delight taste buds.

Ingredients:

- 4 large egg whites, at room temperature
- 1 cup (200 g) granulated sugar
- 1/4 teaspoon (1.25 g) cream of tartar
- 1/2 teaspoon (2.5 ml) vanilla extract
- Food coloring (optional)

Instructions:

-Preheat your oven to 225°F (110°C).

-Line two baking sheets with parchment paper.

-In a clean, dry mixing bowl, beat the egg whites on medium speed using an electric mixer until they become frothy.

-Add the cream of tartar and continue to beat on medium-high speed until soft peaks form.

-Gradually add the granulated sugar, about 1 tablespoon at a time, while continuing to beat the egg whites.

-Once all the sugar is added, increase the mixer speed to high and beat until the meringue is glossy and stiff peaks form. This will take about 5-7 minutes.

-Add the vanilla extract and mix until just combined.

-If using food coloring, add a few drops and gently fold it into the meringue until evenly distributed.

-Transfer the meringue mixture to a piping bag fitted with a large star or round tip.

-Pipe small mounds or rosettes onto the prepared baking sheets, spacing them about 1 inch (2.5 cm) apart.

-Place the baking sheets in the preheated oven and bake for 1.5 to 2 hours, or until the meringues are dry and can be easily lifted off the parchment paper.

-Turn off the oven and let the meringues cool completely in the oven with the door slightly ajar. This will help them dry out and prevent cracking.

-Once completely cooled, store the meringue cookies in an airtight container at room temperature. They will keep well for up to 2 weeks.

Medkit Muffins

Revitalize your snack time with Medkit Muffins, inspired by the lifesaving items in Fortnite. These wholesome muffins are packed with nutritious ingredients like oats, bananas, and berries, providing the perfect boost of energy to keep you going through the day. Moist, flavorful, and easy to make, each muffin is a delightful combination of health and taste, ideal for breakfast, a midday snack, or a quick pick-me-up during gaming sessions. Enjoy the delicious comfort of Medkit Muffins and recharge your body and spirit with every bite.

Ingredients:

- 1 1/2 cups (180 g) whole wheat flour
- 1 cup (240 ml) rolled oats
- 1 teaspoon (5 g) baking soda
- 1/2 teaspoon (2.5 g) baking powder
- 1/2 teaspoon (2.5 g) salt
- 1 teaspoon (5 g) ground cinnamon
- 1/4 teaspoon (1.25 g) ground nutmeg
- 1/2 cup (120 ml) chopped walnuts or pecans
- 3 ripe bananas, mashed
- 2 large eggs
- 1/2 cup (120 ml) Greek yogurt or applesauce
- 1/3 cup (80 ml) honey or maple syrup
- 1/4 cup (60 ml) coconut oil, melted
- 1 teaspoon (5 ml) vanilla extract
- 1/2 cup (120 ml) milk (any kind)

Instructions:

1.Preheat the Oven:

-Preheat your oven to 350°F (175°C). Line a muffin tin with paper liners or lightly grease it.

2.Prepare Dry Ingredients:

-In a large bowl, whisk together the whole wheat flour, rolled oats, baking soda, baking powder, salt, ground cinnamon, ground nutmeg.

-Stir in the chopped walnuts or pecans.

3.Prepare Wet Ingredients:

-In another bowl, combine the mashed bananas, eggs, Greek yogurt (or applesauce), honey (or maple syrup), melted coconut oil, vanilla extract, and milk. Mix well until smooth and well combined.

4.Combine Ingredients:

-Pour the wet ingredients into the bowl with the dry ingredients. Stir gently until just combined. Be careful not to overmix; the batter should be slightly lumpy.

5.Fill Muffin Tins:

-Spoon the batter into the prepared muffin tin, filling each cup about 3/4 full.

6.Bake:

-Bake in the preheated oven for 18-20 minutes, or until a toothpick inserted into the center of a muffin comes out clean.

-Allow the muffins to cool in the tin for about 5 minutes, then transfer them to a wire rack to cool completely.

-These healthy banana-nut muffins can be enjoyed warm or at room temperature. You can wrap them with a red cross band to resemble the Medkit item.

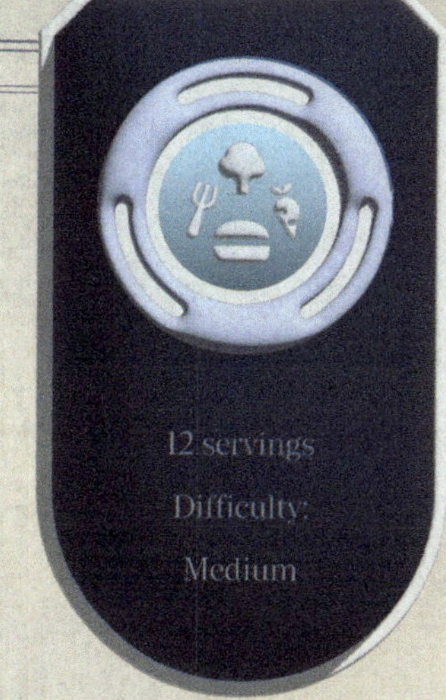

Mini Shield Cupcakes

Power up your dessert game with Mini Shield Cupcakes, inspired by the essential shields in Fortnite. These delightful cupcakes are topped with a vibrant blue frosting, mimicking the look of the game's shield potions. Moist and fluffy, each cupcake is a sweet treat that packs a punch of flavor, perfect for parties, gaming nights, or just indulging your sweet tooth. Decorate them with sprinkles or candy to add an extra layer of fun and creativity. Enjoy the delicious protection of Mini Shield Cupcakes and keep your energy levels high!

Ingredients:

For the Cupcakes:

- 1 1/2 cups (180 g) all-purpose flour
- 1 teaspoon (5 g) baking powder
- 1/2 teaspoon (2.5 g) baking soda
- 1/4 teaspoon (1.25 g) salt
- 1/2 cup (115 g) unsalted butter, softened
- 3/4 cup (150 g) granulated sugar
- 2 large eggs
- 1 teaspoon (5 ml) vanilla extract
- 1/2 cup (120 ml) milk
- 1 cup (240 ml) fresh or frozen blueberries

For the Blue Frosting:

- 1/2 cup (115 g) unsalted butter, softened
- 2 cups (240 g) powdered sugar
- 2-3 tablespoons (30-45 ml) milk
- 1 teaspoon (5 ml) vanilla extract
- 3-4 drops blue food coloring
- Blue sprinkles (optional)

Instructions:

-Preheat your oven to 350°F (175°C). Line a mini muffin tin with cupcake liners.

-In a medium bowl, whisk together the flour, baking powder, baking soda, and salt.

-In a large bowl, beat the softened butter and granulated sugar together until light and fluffy.

-Add the eggs one at a time, beating well after each addition. Stir in the vanilla extract.

-Gradually add the dry ingredients to the wet ingredients, alternating with the milk, beginning and ending with the dry ingredients and mix.

-Gently fold in the blueberries.

-Spoon the batter into the prepared mini muffin tin, filling each cup about 3/4 full.

-Bake in the preheated oven for 15-18 minutes, or until a toothpick inserted into the center of a cupcake comes out clean.

-Allow the cupcakes to cool in the tin for 5 minutes, then transfer them to a wire rack to cool completely.

-In a large bowl, beat the softened butter until creamy.

-Gradually add the powdered sugar, one cup at a time and beat well.

-Add the milk and vanilla extract, and beat until the frosting is smooth and fluffy.

-Add 3-4 drops of blue food coloring and mix until the color is evenly distributed. Adjust the amount of food coloring to achieve your desired shade of blue.

-Once the cupcakes are completely cooled, use a piping bag or a knife to frost the cupcakes with the blue frosting and serve!

Peely Foster

Swing into sweetness with Peely Banana Foster, inspired by Fortnite's beloved banana character, Peely. This decadent dessert features ripe bananas sautéed in a rich caramel sauce made from butter, brown sugar, cinnamon, and a splash of rum, then flambéed to perfection. Served over a scoop of vanilla ice cream, each bite offers a warm, gooey, and utterly delightful experience. Perfect for special occasions or a treat-yourself moment, Peely Banana Foster is a show-stopping dessert that brings a tropical twist to your table.

Ingredients:

For the Bananas Foster:

- 4 ripe bananas, peeled and halved lengthwise
- 1/4 cup (60 g) unsalted butter
- 1/2 cup (100 g) brown sugar
- 1 teaspoon (5 g) ground cinnamon
- 1/4 cup (60 ml) banana liqueur (optional)
- 1/4 cup (60 ml) dark rum
- 1 teaspoon (5 ml) vanilla extract

For Serving:

- Vanilla ice cream

Instructions:

1.Prepare the Sauce:

-In a large skillet, melt the butter over medium heat.

-Add the brown sugar and cinnamon, stirring until the sugar dissolves and the mixture is bubbly.

2.Cook the Bananas:

-Place the banana halves in the skillet, cut side down.

-Cook for 2-3 minutes until the bananas start to soften and caramelize.

3.Add the Liquor:

-If using banana liqueur, pour it over the bananas and cook for an additional 1-2 minutes.

-Pour the dark rum over the bananas and carefully ignite it with a long lighter or match. Stand back and let the flames cook off the alcohol, about 1-2 minutes.

4.Finish the Sauce:

-Once the flames subside, add the vanilla extract to the skillet.

-Gently stir the sauce to coat the bananas evenly.

5.Serve:

-Place a scoop of vanilla ice cream in each serving bowl.

-Spoon the bananas and sauce over the ice cream.

Perfect Yogurt Parfait

This delightful parfait layers creamy yogurt with fresh, juicy berries, crunchy granola, and a drizzle of honey, creating a harmonious blend of flavors and textures. Ideal for breakfast, a healthy snack, or a light dessert, each spoonful provides a refreshing and satisfying taste that energizes and delights. Easy to prepare and beautifully presented, the Perfect Yogurt Parfait is a versatile and nutritious treat that's perfect for any time of day.

Ingredients:

- 2 cups (480 ml) Greek yogurt or your preferred yogurt
- 1/4 cup (60 ml) honey or maple syrup (optional, for added sweetness)
- 1 cup (150 g) fresh berries (such as strawberries, blueberries, raspberries, blackberries)
- 1 cup (120 g) granola
- 1 medium banana, sliced (optional)
- 1/2 cup (50 g) chopped nuts (such as almonds, walnuts, or pecans) (optional)
- Fresh mint leaves for garnish (optional)

Instructions:

1.Prepare the Yogurt:

-In a medium bowl, mix the Greek yogurt with honey or maple syrup, if using. Adjust the sweetness to your liking.

2.Layer the Parfait:

-In clear serving glasses or bowls, start by adding a layer of yogurt at the bottom.

-Add a layer of fresh berries on top of the yogurt.

-Add a layer of granola over the berries.

-If using, add a few slices of banana and a sprinkle of chopped nuts.

-Repeat the layers until you reach the top of the glass or bowl, finishing with a layer of yogurt.

3.Garnish and Serve:

-Top the parfait with a few more fresh berries and a sprinkle of granola.

-Garnish with fresh mint leaves if desired.

4.Serve Immediately:

-Serve the yogurt parfaits immediately to enjoy the crunchy texture of the granola. If you prefer a softer granola texture, let the parfait sit for a few minutes before serving.

Polar Peak Pancakes

Embrace the chill and dive into the deliciousness of Polar Peak Pancakes, inspired by the frosty heights of Fortnite's Polar Peak. These fluffy, golden pancakes are stacked high and topped with a snowy drizzle of powdered sugar, a generous pat of butter, and a cascade of warm maple syrup. Perfect for a cozy breakfast or brunch, each bite melts in your mouth, offering a comforting and satisfying start to your day. Add fresh berries or a dollop of whipped cream to elevate this classic dish into a frosty, flavorful delight that brings the magic!

Ingredients:

For the Pancakes:

- 1 1/2 cups (180 g) all-purpose flour
- 3 1/2 teaspoons (15 g) baking powder
- 1 teaspoon (5 g) salt
- 1 tablespoon (15 g) granulated sugar
- 1 1/4 cups (300 ml) milk
- 1 egg
- 3 tablespoons (45 g) unsalted butter, melted
- 1 teaspoon (5 ml) vanilla extract
- 1 cup (150 g) fresh or frozen blueberries

For Serving:

- Maple syrup
- Extra blueberries
- Powdered sugar (optional)
- Butter (optional)

Instructions:

1.Prepare the Batter:

-In a large bowl, sift together the flour, baking powder, salt, and sugar.

-Make a well in the center and pour in the milk, egg, melted butter, and vanilla extract. Mix until smooth.

2.Fold in Blueberries:

-Gently fold the blueberries into the batter, being careful not to overmix.

3.Preheat the Griddle:

-Heat a lightly oiled griddle or frying pan over medium-high heat.

4.Cook the Pancakes:

-Pour or scoop about 1/4 cup (60 ml) of batter for each pancake onto the griddle.

-Cook until bubbles form on the surface and the edges are set, about 2-3 minutes.

-Flip with a spatula and cook until browned on the other side, another 2-3 minutes.

-Adjust the heat as needed to prevent burning and ensure the pancakes cook through.

5.Keep Warm:

-Transfer cooked pancakes to a baking sheet and keep warm in a low oven (about 200°F / 95°C) until all the pancakes are cooked.

6.Serve:

-Stack the pancakes on plates.

-Drizzle with maple syrup and top with extra blueberries.

-Optionally, add a dusting of powdered sugar and a pat of butter on top

.

Unreal Pistachio Mousse

Elevate your dessert game with Unreal Pistachio Mousse, inspired by the extraordinary and surreal experiences in Fortnite. This luxurious mousse is light, airy, and packed with the rich, nutty flavor of pistachios, offering a taste that's both sophisticated and delightful. Topped with a sprinkle of chopped pistachios and a dollop of whipped cream, each spoonful delivers a creamy and dreamy indulgence.

Ingredients:

- 1 cup (120 g) shelled pistachios, plus extra for garnish
- 2 tablespoons (25 g) granulated sugar
- 2 cups (480 ml) heavy cream
- 1/2 cup (120 ml) whole milk
- 1/4 cup (50 g) granulated sugar
- 3 large egg yolks
- 1 teaspoon (5 ml) vanilla extract
- 1 tablespoon (10 g) powdered gelatin
- 2 tablespoons (30 ml) cold water

Instructions:

1.Prepare the Pistachios:

-Place the shelled pistachios and 2 tablespoons of granulated sugar in a food processor. Process until finely ground.

2.Prepare the Gelatin:

-In a small bowl, sprinkle the powdered gelatin over 2 tablespoons of cold water. Let it sit for about 5 minutes to bloom.

3.Prepare the Pistachio Base:

-In a medium saucepan, combine the ground pistachios, whole milk, and 1/4 cup granulated sugar. Heat over medium heat until the mixture is hot but not boiling, stirring frequently.

-In a separate bowl, whisk the egg yolks. Gradually add a small amount of the hot pistachio mixture to the egg yolks, whisking constantly to temper the eggs. Then, pour the tempered egg yolk mixture back into the saucepan with the remaining pistachio mixture.

-Cook over medium heat, stirring constantly, until the mixture thickens and coats the back of a spoon. Do not let it boil.

4.Add the Gelatin:

-Remove the saucepan from heat and stir in the bloomed gelatin until it is fully dissolved. Add the vanilla extract and mix well.

-Allow the mixture to cool to room temperature.

5.Whip the Cream:

-In a large mixing bowl, whip the heavy cream until soft peaks form.

6.Fold in the Whipped Cream:

-Once the pistachio mixture has cooled, gently fold in the whipped cream until fully combined and smooth.

7.Chill the Mousse and serve.

Beverages

Boogie Drink

Elevate your dessert game with Unreal Pistachio Mousse, inspired by the extraordinary and surreal experiences in Fortnite. This luxurious mousse is light, airy, and packed with the rich, nutty flavor of pistachios, offering a taste that's both sophisticated and delightful. Topped with a sprinkle of chopped pistachios and a dollop of whipped cream, each spoonful delivers a creamy and dreamy indulgence.

Ingredients:

For the Drink:

- 1 cup (240 ml) orange juice
- 1 cup (240 ml) pineapple juice
- 1/2 cup (120 ml) lemon juice (about 2-3 lemons)
- 1/2 cup (120 ml) lime juice (about 4-5 limes)
- 1/2 cup (120 ml) grenadine syrup
- 2 cups (480 ml) soda water or sparkling water
- Ice cubes

For Garnish:

- Orange slices
- Pineapple chunks
- Lemon slices
- Lime slices
- Fresh mint leaves
- Maraschino cherries

Instructions:

1.Prepare the Drink Mixture:

-In a large pitcher, combine the orange juice, pineapple juice, lemon juice, lime juice, and grenadine syrup. Stir well to mix.

2.Add Fizz:

-Just before serving, gently stir in the soda water or sparkling water to add a fizzy touch.

3.Serve the Drink:

-Fill glasses with ice cubes.

-Pour the Boogie Bomb Drink over the ice.

4.Garnish:

-Garnish each glass with orange slices, pineapple chunks, lemon slices, lime slices, fresh mint leaves, and maraschino cherries.

Chug Jug Smoothie

Recharge and refresh with the Chug Jug Smoothie, inspired by the essential health potion in Fortnite. This vibrant blue smoothie is packed with nutritious ingredients, providing a delicious and energizing boost to start your day or refuel after a game. The combination of blueberries, banana, Greek yogurt, and a hint of honey creates a creamy and satisfying drink that's as tasty as it is healthy.

Ingredients:

- 1 cup (240 ml) fresh or frozen blueberries
- 1 banana
- 1/2 cup (120 ml) Greek yogurt
- 1/2 cup (120 ml) milk (or any plant-based milk)
- 1 tablespoon (15 ml) honey or maple syrup
- 1/2 teaspoon (2.5 ml) vanilla extract
- 1/4 cup (60 ml) water or coconut water
- A handful of ice cubes
- A pinch of blue spirulina powder (optional, for a more vibrant blue color)
- Fresh mint leaves for garnish

Instructions:

1.Prepare the Ingredients:

-If using fresh blueberries, rinse them thoroughly. If using frozen blueberries, no need to thaw.

-Peel the banana and break it into smaller pieces for easier blending.

2.Blend the Smoothie:

-In a blender, combine the blueberries, banana, Greek yogurt, milk, honey (or maple syrup), vanilla extract, and water (or coconut water).

-Add a handful of ice cubes to make the smoothie more refreshing and cold.

-If you want a more vibrant blue color, add a pinch of blue spirulina powder. This is optional but can give your smoothie that extra Fortnite Chug Jug look.

3.Blend Until Smooth:

-Blend all the ingredients on high speed until the mixture is smooth and creamy. If the smoothie is too thick, you can add a bit more water or milk to achieve your desired consistency.

4.Serve:

-Pour the smoothie into a glass. For a more authentic Chug Jug feel, you can serve it in a mason jar or a glass bottle with a straw.

-Garnish with fresh mint leaves for a refreshing touch.

5.Enjoy:

-Your Chug Jug Smoothie is ready to be enjoyed. This smoothie is not only delicious but also packed with antioxidants, vitamins, and energy to keep you going through your day, much like a real Fortnite Chug Jug!

Shield Potion Shake

Power up with the Shield Potion Shake, inspired by Fortnite's iconic shield potion. This vibrant blue shake is a fun and delicious treat that combines the creamy richness of vanilla ice cream with a splash of color. Perfect for cooling down and recharging, this shake is sure to be a hit with gamers and dessert lovers alike.

Ingredients:

- 2 cups (480 ml) vanilla ice cream
- 1 cup (240 ml) milk (whole milk for creamier texture)
- 1 teaspoon (5 ml) vanilla extract
- 3-4 drops blue food coloring
- Whipped cream (for topping)
- Blue sprinkles or sugar crystals (for garnish)
- Blue straws (optional)

Instructions:

1.Prepare the Milkshake Base:

-In a blender, combine the vanilla ice cream, milk, and vanilla extract. Blend until smooth and creamy.

2.Add the Blue Color:

-Add 3-4 drops of blue food coloring to the blender. Blend again until the color is evenly distributed and you have a vibrant blue milkshake. You can adjust the amount of food coloring to achieve your desired shade of blue.

3.Chill the Glasses:

-For an extra touch, chill the glasses in the freezer for a few minutes before serving. This will help keep your shake cold longer and enhance the presentation.

4.Serve the Shake:

-Pour the blue vanilla milkshake into the chilled glasses.

5.Top with Whipped Cream:

-Generously top each shake with whipped cream. This adds a fun and indulgent touch to your Shield Potion Shake.

6.Garnish:

-Sprinkle blue sprinkles or sugar crystals on top of the whipped cream for an extra decorative effect.

7.Optional Extras:

-Add a blue straw to complete the look and make it easier to drink.

8.Enjoy:

-Your Shield Potion Shake is ready to be enjoyed. This rich and creamy vanilla milkshake, colored in a vibrant blue, is a perfect Fortnite-themed treat that looks just like the iconic Shield Potion.

Slurp Juice

Quench your thirst and boost your energy with Slurp Juice, inspired by the rejuvenating potion from Fortnite. This refreshing drink combines the tartness of lemon juice with the sweetness of blue raspberries, making it a perfect cool-down beverage. Whether you're taking a break from gaming or just need a delicious refreshment, Slurp Juice is a vibrant and healthy choice.

Ingredients:

- 1 cup (240 ml) fresh or frozen blue raspberries (or substitute with regular raspberries and a few drops of blue food coloring)
- 1/2 cup (120 ml) freshly squeezed lemon juice (about 2-3 lemons)
- 1/4 cup (60 ml) honey or agave syrup
- 2 cups (480 ml) cold water
- 1 cup (240 ml) sparkling water
- A handful of fresh mint leaves
- Ice cubes
- Blue spirulina powder (optional, for a more vibrant blue color)
- Lemon slices and mint sprigs for garnish

Instructions:

1.Prepare the Blue Raspberry Base:

-If using fresh blue raspberries, rinse them thoroughly. If using frozen raspberries, allow them to thaw slightly.

-In a blender, combine the blue raspberries and honey (or agave syrup). Blend until smooth.

2.Strain the Mixture:

-Pour the blended raspberry mixture through a fine mesh strainer into a large pitcher to remove the seeds, using a spoon to press the liquid through. If you're using regular raspberries, add a few drops of blue food coloring to achieve the blue hue.

3.Mix the Lemonade:

-Add the freshly squeezed lemon juice and cold water to the pitcher. Stir well to combine.

-For a more vibrant blue color, you can add a pinch of blue spirulina powder at this stage. This is optional but will enhance the visual appeal.

4.Add Mint Twist:

-Tear a handful of fresh mint leaves and add them to the pitcher. Using a spoon or muddler, gently press the mint leaves to release their flavor.

5.Chill the Slurp Juice:

-Add ice cubes to the pitcher to chill the lemonade. Let it sit for a few minutes to allow the flavors to meld together.

6.Add Sparkling Water:

-Just before serving, add the sparkling water to the pitcher. This will give your Slurp Juice a refreshing fizz.

-Pour the Slurp Juice into glasses filled with ice cubes. Garnish with lemon slices and mint sprigs for an extra touch of freshness.

Storm Surge Drink

Get ready to ride the wave of flavor with the Storm Surge Drink, a vibrant and refreshing mango smoothie inspired by the intense energy of Fortnite's storm surge. This smoothie is packed with the tropical sweetness of ripe mangoes, balanced with a hint of citrus and creamy yogurt, making it the perfect drink to cool you down and keep you energized.

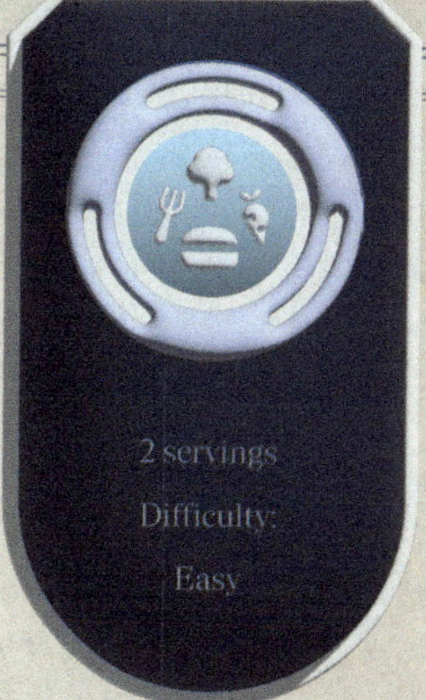

2 servings

Difficulty: Easy

Ingredients:

- 2 large ripe mangoes, peeled, pitted, and chopped
- 1 cup (240 ml) Greek yogurt
- 1/2 cup (120 ml) coconut milk or any milk of your choice
- 1 tablespoon (15 ml) honey or maple syrup (optional, for added sweetness)
- 1 teaspoon (5 ml) vanilla extract (optional)
- 1 cup (150 g) ice cubes (optional, for a thicker texture)
- Fresh mint leaves or a lime wedge for garnish (optional)

Instructions:

1.Prepare the Ingredients:

-Peel, pit, and chop the mangoes. Place them in a blender.

2.Blend the Smoothie:

-Add the Greek yogurt, coconut milk, honey or maple syrup (if using), and vanilla extract (if using) to the blender.

-Blend on high speed until smooth and creamy. If you prefer a thicker texture, add ice cubes and blend again until smooth.

3.Adjust Consistency and Sweetness:

-Taste the smoothie and adjust the sweetness by adding more honey or maple syrup if desired.

-If the smoothie is too thick, add a little more coconut milk and blend again until you reach the desired consistency.

4.Serve:

-Pour the mango smoothie into glasses.

-Garnish with fresh mint leaves or a lime wedge, if desired.

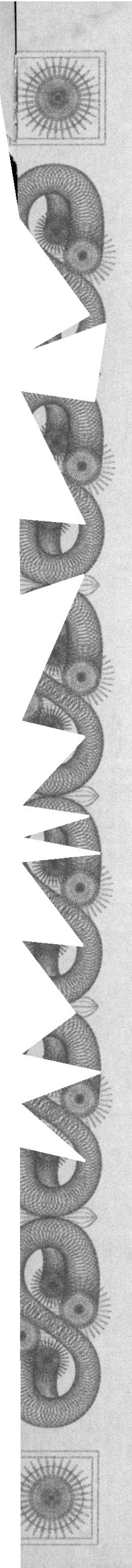

Wollseif Media
Richardstraße 112, 12043 Berlin
info@wollseif.com

Author
Onur Duman

Art Director
Berkin Yeşil

Editor
Öykü Özmakinacı

Cover design by Mehmet Yunus Çoban

ISBN: 978-3-9824791-4-9

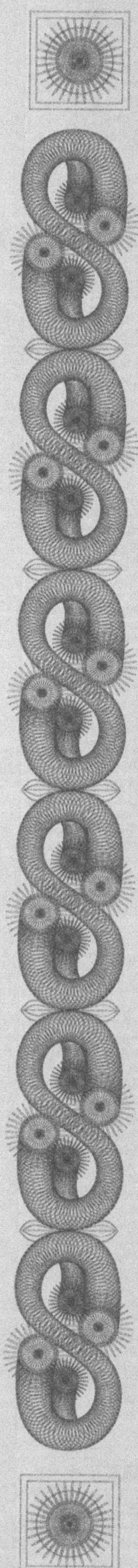

Made in the USA
Las Vegas, NV
16 December 2024

14539307R10077